Stealing Elections

Stealing Elections

How Voter Fraud
Threatens Our Democracy

JOHN FUND

ENCOUNTER BOOKS
SAN FRANCISCO

First edition published in 2004 by Encounter Books, an activity of Encounter for Culture and Education, Inc., a nonprofit tax exempt corporation.

Encounter Books website address: www.encounterbooks.com

Manufactured in the United States and printed on acid-free paper.

The paper used in this publication meets the minimum requirements of ANSI/NISO Z39.48-1992 (R 1997)(*Permanence of Paper*).

Library of Congress Cataloging-in-Publication Data

Fund, John.
   Stealing elections : how voter fraud threatens our democracy / john fund.
     p. cm.
   Includes index.
   ISBN 1-59403-061-8 (alk. paper)
     1. Elections—Corrupt practices—United States. 2. Political corruption 3. United States I. Title.
   JK1994 .F86 2004
   324.973'0931—dc22   2004057055

10 9 8 7 6 5 4 3 2 1

For Mom and Dad—they taught me to learn about the world without forgetting where I came from.

Contents

★ Democracy Imperiled

O ur nation may be on the brink of repeating the 2000 Florida election debacle, though this time not in one, but in several states, with allegations of voter fraud, intimidation and manipulation of voting machines added to the generalized chaos that sent our last presidential contest into overtime. There is still time to reduce the chance of another electoral meltdown, both this year and in future years. But this will not happen unless we acknowledge that the United States has a haphazard, fraud-prone election system befitting an emerging Third World country rather than the world's leading democracy.

With its hanging chads, butterfly ballots and Supreme Court intervention, the Florida fiasco compelled this country to confront an ugly reality: that we have been making do with what noted political scientist Walter Dean Burnham has called "the modern world's sloppiest electoral systems." How sloppy? Lethally so. At least eight of the nineteen hijackers who attacked the World Trade Center and the Pentagon were actually able to register to vote in either Virginia or Florida while they made their deadly preparations for 9/11.

The 2000 recount was more than merely a national embarrassment; it left a lasting scar on the American electoral psyche. A recent Zogby poll found that 38 percent of Americans still regard the 2000 election outcome as questionable. Many Republicans believe that Democratic judges on the Florida Supreme Court tried to hand their state to Al Gore based on selective partisan recounts and the illegal votes of felons and aliens. Many Democrats feel that the justices of the U.S. Supreme Court tilted toward Bush, and they refuse to accept his victory as valid. But this issue transcends "red state" vs. "blue state" partisan grievances. Many Americans are convinced that politicians can't be trusted to play by the rules and will either commit fraud or intimidate voters at the slightest opportunity.

Indeed, the level of suspicion has grown so dramatically that it threatens to undermine our political system. Nearly 10 percent of Americans believe their votes are not counted accurately, and almost as many worry that this is the case, according to a July 2004 poll by John Zogby. A Rasmussen Research poll in June found that 44 percent of Americans were either very or somewhat worried that a Florida-style mess could happen again in 2004. This growing cynicism diminishes respect for the nation's institutions and lowers voter participation. Only 11 percent of the 18- to 19-year-olds eligible to vote for the first time now bother to go to the polls. The United States ranks 139th out of 163 democracies in the rate of voter participation. The more that voting is left to the zealous or self-interested few, the more we see harshly personal campaigns that dispense with any positive vision of our national future. "If this escalates, we're in horrendous shape as a country," says Curtis Gans, who runs the Committee for the Study of the American Electorate. "If election results are followed by lawsuits, appeals, fire and counterfire, many people who are already saying to hell with the process are going to exit."

The 2000 election resulted in some modest reforms at the federal level such as the Help America Vote Act of 2002, but the implementation has been so slow. Only $670 million of the promised $3.9 billion in grants to upgrade technology, cull voter rolls and enhance training had been dispersed to the states as of May 2004. This means that the nation's voting systems will be in no better shape this November than they were in 2000, when about 2 percent of all votes for president nationwide weren't counted for one reason or another, the vast majority because of voter error or outdated machines.

America's election problems go beyond the strapped budgets of many local election offices. More insidious are flawed voter rolls, voter ignorance, lackadaisical law enforcement and a shortage of trained volunteers. All this adds up to an open invitation for errors, miscounts or fraud.

Reform is easy to talk about, but difficult to bring about. Many of the suggested improvements, such as requiring voters to show ID at the polls, are bitterly opposed. For instance, Maria Cardona, spokeswoman for the Democratic National Committee, claims that "ballot security and preventing voter fraud are just code words for voter intimidation and suppression." Even improved technology is controversial. This November, around fifty million Americans will be using electronic voting machines similar to ATM machines, and some computer scientists are alarmed by the possibility that hackers could change the software to cast multiple votes or do other kinds of mischief. Both Democratic senator Hillary Clinton and GOP representative Steve King of Iowa are backing separate pieces of legislation to require that machines issue paper receipts for voters to verify before casting their ballots. But the legislation hasn't even had a hearing and only Nevada will have paper receipts in place by the fall 2004 election.

Confusion and claims of fraud are likely this time around, especially if the election is as close as it was in 2000. Can the nation take another Florida-style controversy?

Indeed, we may be on the way to turning Election Day into Election Month through a new legal quagmire: election by litigation. Every close race now carries with it the prospect of demands for recounts, lawsuits and seating challenges in Congress. "We're waiting for the day that pols can just cut out the middleman and settle all elections in court," jokes Chuck Todd, editor of the political tip sheet *Hotline*. Such gallows humor may be entirely appropriate given the predicament we face. The 2000 election may have marked a permanent change in how elections can be decided, much as the battle over the Supreme Court nomination of Robert Bork changed, apparently forever, the politics of judicial appointments. On April 19, 2004, Senator John Kerry campaigned in Florida with Senator Joe Lieberman, the 2000 Democratic vice presidential candidate, and vowed— six months before a single ballot was cast, counted or disputed—that he was ready to take the 2004 election to court. "We are going to bring legal challenge to those districts that make it difficult for people to register. We're going to bring challenge to those people that disen-roll people," he told a rally. "And we're going to challenge any place in America where you cannot trace the vote and count the votes of Americans. Period!" Democrats plan to have over ten thousand lawyers on the ground in all states this November, ready for action if the election is close and they see a way to contest it. "If you think of election problems as akin to forest fires, the woods are no drier than they were in 2000, but many more people have matches," says Doug Chapin of Electionline.org, an Internet clearinghouse of election news. If the trend toward litigation continues, winners in the future may have to hope not only that they win but that their margins are beyond "the margin of litigation."

Some of the sloppiness that makes fraud and foul-ups in election counts possible seems to be built into the system by design. The National Voter Registration Act ("Motor Voter Law"), the first law signed into law by President Clinton upon entering office, imposed fraud-friendly rules on the states by requiring driver's license bureaus to register anyone applying for licenses, to offer mail-in registration with no identification needed, and to forbid government workers to challenge new registrants, while making it difficult to purge "dead-wood" voters (those who have died or moved away). In 2001, the voter rolls in many American cities included more names than the U.S. Census listed as the total number of residents over age eight-een. Philadelphia's voter rolls, for instance, have jumped 24 percent since 1995 at the same time that the city's population has declined by 13 percent. CBS's *60 Minutes* created a stir in 1999 when it found people in California using mail-in forms to register fictitious peo-ple, or pets, and then obtaining absentee ballots in their names. By this means, for example, the illegal alien who assassinated the Mex-ican presidential candidate Luis Donaldo Colosio was registered to vote in San Pedro, California—twice.

Ironically, Mexico and many other countries have election systems that are far more secure than ours. To obtain voter creden-tials, the citizen must present a photo, write a signature and give a thumbprint. The voter card includes a picture with a hologram covering it, a magnetic strip and a serial number to guard against tampering. To cast a ballot, voters must present the card and be certified by a thumbprint scanner. This system was instrumental in allowing the 2000 election of Vicente Fox, the first opposition party candidate to be elected president in seventy years.

But in the United States, at a time of heightened security and mundane rules that require citizens to show ID to travel and even rent a video, only seventeen states require some form of documentation in order to vote. "Why should the important process of voting be the one exception to this rule?" asks Karen Saranita, a former fraud investigator for a Democratic state senator in California. Americans agree. A Rasmussen Research poll finds that 82 percent of Americans, including 75 percent of Democrats, believe that "people should be required to show a driver's license or some other form of photo ID before they are allowed to vote."

The reason for such support is that citizens instinctively realize that some people will be tempted to cut corners in the cutthroat world of politics. "Some of the world's most clever people are attracted to politics, because that's where the power is," says University of Virginia political scientist Larry Sabato. "So they're always going to be one step ahead of the law."

Election fraud, whether it's phony voter registrations, illegal absentee ballots, shady recounts or old-fashioned ballot-box stuffing, can be found in every part of the United States, although it is probably spreading because of the ever-so-tight divisions that have polarized the country and created so many close elections lately. Although most fraud is found in urban areas, there are current scandals in rural South Dakota and Texas. In recent years, Baltimore, Philadelphia, New Orleans and Milwaukee have all had election-related scandals. Wisconsin officials convicted a New York heiress working for Al Gore of giving homeless people cigarettes if they rode in a van to the polls and voted. The *Miami Herald* won a Pulitzer Prize in 1999 for uncovering how "vote brokers" employed by candidate Xavier Suarez stole a mayoral election in Miami by tampering with 4,740 absentee ballots. Many were cast by homeless people who didn't live in the city and were paid $10 apiece and shuttled to the elections office in vans. All of the absentee ballots were thrown out by a court four months later and Mr. Suarez's opponent Joe Carollo was installed as mayor.

But such interventions are rare, even when fraud is proven. In 1997, the House of Representatives voted along partisan lines to demand that the Justice Department prosecute Hermandad Mexicana Nacional, a group that investigators for the House Administration Committee say registered hundreds of illegal voters in a razor-thin congressional race in Orange County, California. But federal immigration officials refused to cooperate with the probe, citing "privacy" concerns, and nothing was done beyond yanking a federal contract that paid Hermandad to conduct citizenship classes. The same year, a U.S. Senate probe into fraud in a Senate race in Louisiana found more than 1,500 cases in which two voters used the same Social Security number. But further investigations collapsed after Democratic senators walked off the probe, calling it unfair, and then Attorney General Janet Reno removed FBI agents from the case because the probe wasn't "bipartisan."

A note about partisanship: Since Democrats figure prominently in the vast majority of examples of election fraud described in this book, some readers will jump to the conclusion that this is a one-sided attack on a single party. I do not believe Republicans are inherently more virtuous or honest than anyone else in politics, and I myself often vote Libertarian or independent. Voter fraud occurs in both Republican strongholds such as Kentucky hollows and Democratic bastions such as New Orleans. When Republicans operated political machines such as Philadelphia's Meehan dynasty up until 1951 or the patronage mill of Nassau County, New York, until the 1990s, they were fully capable of bending—and breaking—the rules. Earl Mazo, the journalist who exhaustively documented the election fraud in Richard J. Daley's Chicago that may have handed Illinois to John F. Kennedy in the photo-finish 1960 election, says there was also "definitely fraud" in downstate Republican counties "but they didn't have the votes to counterbalance Chicago."

While they have not had the control of local and administrative offices necessary to tilt the rules improperly in their favor, Republicans have at times been guilty of intimidation tactics designed to discourage voting. In the 1980s, the Republican National Committee hired off-duty policemen to monitor polling places in New Jersey and Louisiana in the neighborhoods of minority voters, until the outcry forced them to sign a consent decree forswearing all such "ballot security" programs in the future.

In their book *Dirty Little Secrets*, Larry Sabato and co-author Glenn Simpson of the *Wall Street Journal* noted another factor in why Republican election fraud is less common. Republican base voters are middle-class and not easily induced to commit fraud, while "the pool of people who appear to be available and more vulnerable to an invitation to participate in vote fraud tend to lean Democratic." Some liberal activists that Sabato and Simpson interviewed even partly justified fraudulent electoral behavior on the grounds that because the poor and dispossessed have so little political clout, "extraordinary measures (for example, stretching the absentee ballot or registration rules) are required to compensate." Paul Herrnson, director of the Center for American Politics at the University of Maryland, agrees that "most incidents of wide-scale voter fraud reportedly occur in inner cities, which are largely populated by minority groups."

Democrats are far more skilled at encouraging poor people— who need money—to participate in shady vote-buying schemes. "I had no choice. I was hungry that day," Thomas Felder told the *Miami Herald* in explaining why he illegally voted in the Suarez-Carollo mayoral election. "You wanted the money, you were told who to vote for." Sometimes it's not just food that vote stealers are hungry for. A former Democratic congressman gave me this explanation of why voting irregularities more often crop up in his party's back yard: "When many Republicans lose an election, they go back into what they call the private sector. When many Democrats lose an election, they lose power and money. They need to eat, and people will do an awful lot in order to eat."

Investigations of voter fraud are inherently political; and because they often involve race, they are often not zealously pursued or prosecuted. Attorney General John Ashcroft did launch a Voting Integrity Initiative in 2002, which dramatically reduced both Republican allegations of fraud and Democratic complaints of suppressed minority votes. But many federal and state prosecutors remain leery of tackling fraud or intimidation. After extensive research, I can report that while voting irregularities are common, the number of people who have spent time in jail as a result of a conviction for voter fraud in the last dozen years can be counted on the fingers of one hand.

The U.S. attorney for the Northern District of Louisiana, Donald Washington, admits that "most of the time, we can't do much of anything [about ballot-box improprieties] until the election is over. And the closer we get to the election, the less willing we are to get involved because of just the appearance of impropriety, just the appearance of the federal government somehow shading how this election ought to occur." Several prosecutors told me they fear charges of racism or of a return to Jim Crow voter suppression tactics if they pursue touchy fraud cases. Wade Henderson of the Leadership Conference on Civil Rights calls efforts to fight election fraud "a solution in search of a problem" and "a warmed-over plan for voter intimidation."

But when voters are disfranchised by the counting of improperly cast ballots or outright fraud, their civil rights are violated just as surely as if they were prevented from voting. The integrity of the ballot box is just as important to the credibility of elections as access to it. Voting irregularities have a long pedigree in America, stretching back to the founding of the nation—though most people thought the "bad old days" had ended in 1948 after pistol-packing Texas sheriffs helped stuff Ballot Box 13, stealing a U.S. Senate seat and setting Lyndon Johnson on his road to the White House. Then came the 2004 primary election, when Representative Ciro Rodriguez, a Democrat, charged that during a recount, a missing ballot box appeared in south Texas with enough votes to make his opponent the Democratic nominee by 58 votes.

Political bosses such as Richard J. Daley or George Wallace may have died, but they have successors. A one-party machine in Hawaii intimidates critics and journalists who question its vote harvesting among noncitizens. In 1998, a former Democratic congressman named Austin Murphy was convicted in Pennsylvania of absentee ballot fraud. The Democratic county supervisor who uncovered this scandal, Sean Cavanaugh, was so ostracized by his party that he re-registered as an independent.

Even after Florida 2000, the media tend to downplay or ignore stories of election incompetence, manipulation or theft. Allowing such abuses to vanish into an informational black hole in effect legitimates them. The refusal to insist on simple procedural changes, such as requiring a photo ID at the polls, combined with secure technology and more vigorous prosecutions accelerates our drift toward banana-republic elections.

In 2002, Miami election officials hired the Center for Democracy, which normally observes voting in places like Guatemala or Albania, to send twenty election monitors to south Florida. In 2004, there will be even more observers on the ground. Scrutinizing our own elections the way we have traditionally scrutinized voting in developing countries is, unfortunately, a step in the right direction. But before we can get the clearer laws and better protections we need to deal with fraud and voter mishaps, we have to get a sense of the magnitude of the problem we face.

"Al Gore won the popular vote. I did my job. I did get that vote out. Unfortunately, I didn't get to count it."
—Donna Brazile, Al Gore's campaign manager

CHAPTER ONE

A Conflict of Visions

Pollster John Zogby has spent a lot of time analyzing Americans' attitudes toward our electoral system, particularly in the aftermath of the 2000 Florida fiasco. The picture his polls draw is one of suspicion and cynicism. In a sample of 1,008 likely voters in June 2004, Zogby found that 9 percent of Americans don't believe their votes are counted accurately and another 8 percent aren't sure. Among African Americans, fully 18 percent are skeptical, and among Hispanics the figure is 13 percent. Nor is Zogby alone in sensing the disillusionment of the American electorate. A Rasmussen Research poll conducted for this book found that only 57 percent of Americans believe our elections are fair.

The percentages were up sharply from November 2000, *after* what was arguably the most contentious vote count in our history, when only 3 percent said they didn't think their vote was counted. "There is a worrying element of paranoia," Zogby says. "It's way more a perception than the reality, but we were treated to the sausage-making of elections in 2000 and it wasn't pretty." He himself admits there certainly are gaps in the proper conduct of elections. He remembers doing a study of local election practices for the League of Women Voters in the 1980s and visiting a precinct in his hometown of Utica, New York. After the polls closed at 9:00 PM, workers spent seven minutes noting down the tallies from the lever machines. "Then one of the workers brought out this big cardboard box filled with absentee ballots," Zogby recalls. "The chief worker said, 'To hell with the absentee ballots, we've been working for fifteen hours straight. Let's go home.' They then called in the final results to the elections office and left."

Many people believe this kind of thing still happens on a massive scale and in a calculated fashion. When John Kerry addressed a large, predominantly black audience in Indianapolis in July 2004, he said his campaign would "speak truth to power" in addressing President Bush: "Don't tell us disenfranchising a million African Americans and stealing their votes is the best we can do. This time, in 2004, not only will every vote count—we're going to make sure that every vote is counted." Kerry invoked the ghost of "disfranchisement" just a few days after the immediate past chairman of the Congressional Black Caucus, Representative Eddie Bernice Johnson of Texas, joined with a dozen other House members and asked U.N. Secretary-General Kofi Annan to appoint a delegation to determine if the United States is capable of running its own presidential election.

In a letter to Annan, Representative Johnson and her colleagues wrote: "We are deeply concerned that the right of U.S. citizens to vote in free and fair elections is again in jeopardy." They asked for "international election monitors" to watch for "questionable practices and voter disenfranchisement." To his credit, Annan, perhaps recognizing the partisanship behind the Johnson letter, replied that the United Nations had no jurisdiction. But even though the issue was only a blip on the screen of the rolling presidential campaign of spring 2004, it showed that some political leaders are already laying the groundwork to claim that the 2004 election was "stolen."

It's clear that the two major parties are separated not just by political disagreements but by a basic difference in how they see voting. Democrats gravitate to the view that the most important value is empowering people to exercise their democratic rights. The DNC's Voting Rights Institute emphasizes the need "to remove every barrier that impedes or denies an eligible vote." High in the Democratic Party's pantheon of heroes (even more than they were forty years ago) are "activists from all over America who converged on Mississippi in the summer of 1964 to help educate and register tens of thousands of previously disenfranchised American citizens."

Republicans tend to pay more attention to the rule of law and the standards and procedures that govern elections. Conservative legal scholars have noted that voters as well as election officials have an obligation to make sure that democracy works. Republicans also worry publicly about the upcoming presidential election, but for different reasons. "Illegal aliens, homeless people and vote brokers who bus people from polling place to polling place will all figure in this election," said Rush Limbaugh on his national radio show. Republicans have their own legal team to combat fake voter registrations, absentee ballot fraud and residents of nursing homes being "assisted" more than necessary to cast votes. In June 2004, Ed Gillespie, chairman of the Republican National Committee, sent a letter to Terry McAuliffe, his Democratic counterpart, suggesting that they find ways the two parties could work together to protect the integrity of the election process. One of his ideas was that in close battleground states, each party identify precincts where it fears there might be problems on Election Day. "Each of us would be responsible for recruiting a volunteer for each named precinct," Gillespie wrote. "Similarly bipartisan teams would be assigned to cover multiple precincts to respond to and investigate reports of problems. The teams would agree on avenues of appeals that could be taken to the courts, if needed." Journalists could be embedded with the teams, *à la* the Iraq war, to report on developments.

Parrying and thrusting in this verbal fencing match, McAuliffe wrote back to say that while he "strongly opposed any fraudulent behavior or activity at polling places," the real issue was having the Justice Department ensure that no voter was harassed or intimidated. He dismissed Gillespie's idea of a joint task force to police polling places as "a public relations gambit."

Some Democratic Party allies have had even harsher things to say about Republican efforts to police the polls. Wade Henderson of the Leadership Conference on Civil Rights contends that such actions "serve no useful purpose other than to prevent people from voting" and that the Justice Department's antifraud efforts are really a strategy to scare voters away from the polls. Liberal legal groups are suing to set aside laws in some of the states that require photo ID at the polls on the grounds they discriminate against the poor and minorities.

Clearly the nature and conduct of our elections have become a highly polarized political issue. Getting the parties to agree on anything in the heat of a bitter election season is well-nigh impossible. Al Gore's decision to contest the Florida election in 2000 until the bitter end may have permanently changed the way close elections are decided and cast a cloud over the Bush presidency that never lifted, even during the brief moment of national unity following 9/11. If the 2004 election and future presidential contests are close, the doubts that have collected around the way we vote (and count our votes) could guarantee endless lawsuits and recriminations that will poison public opinion and create a climate of illegitimacy around any final winner.

A Clash of Worldviews

In his classic 1988 book *A Conflict of Visions: The Ideological Origins of Political Struggles*, economist Thomas Sowell outlined how important social "visions" are to many people. By "visions" he meant different senses of how the world works. For decades, public opinion researchers sought the perfect polling question that best correlated with whether someone considered himself a Republican or a Democrat. In the 1960s, Gallup finally came up with the question that has had the most consistent predictive power over the last forty years. It is this: "In your opinion, which is more often to blame if a person is poor? Lack of effort on his own part, or circumstances beyond his control?" Today, as might be expected of a nation divided 50–50 politically, these two competing views on what creates poverty are equally strong.

Competing visions or worldviews are particularly powerful in determining how people think about issues because, unlike "class interests" or other motivating forces, they are largely invisible, even—or especially—to those who have them. They explain how so often in life the same people continually line up on the same sides of different issues. Sowell claims that conflicts of visions dominate history: "We will do almost anything for our visions, except think about them."

Sowell identifies two distinctly different visions. The first he calls the "unconstrained" vision of human nature and the second he terms the "constrained" vision. Those with an unconstrained vision think that if we want a society where people are enlightened, prosperous and equal, we must develop programs and work to implement them. They focus on results or outcomes. That would include making sure as many people as possible vote, as a way of animating the ideals of democracy.

Sometimes that desire to expand voting opportunities takes on unrealistic qualities. The San Francisco Board of Supervisors has placed a measure on the November 2004 ballot that would allow noncitizens to vote in school board elections. "Candidates who run for school board ought to have to campaign in immigrant communities that are filling the public schools with kids," says Supervisor Matt Gonzalez, the proposal's chief sponsor. But city attorney Louise Renne, a Democrat, is adamant that state law probably bars noncitizens from voting on anything until they actually become citizens. "What's next? Osama bin Laden voting?" she asks.

Those with a "constrained" vision of human nature, on the other hand, believe that the goal of reason, rather than remodeling society, should be simply identifying "natural laws" and working within them. Such people focus on general rules and processes. In the area of elections, the constrained vision would favor setting up procedures to make certain that votes are counted accurately and fairly, but not bending these procedures to increase voter participation.

During the 2000 Florida recount I came across many people who represented each of these conflicting visions. At a Jesse Jackson rally, the crowd chanted "Count Every Vote!" and "One Ballot Is One Vote." Meanwhile, many Republicans I met carried a brochure from the Florida Department of Law Enforcement that outlined "Voter Responsibilities." It read in part:

Each registered voter in this state should:
1. Familiarize himself or herself with the candidates and issues.
2. Maintain with the supervisor of elections a current address.
3. Know the location of his or her polling place and its hours.
4. Bring proper identification to the polls.

5. Familiarize himself or herself with the voting equipment in his or her precinct.
6. Make sure that his or her completed ballot is correct.

"I run into two kinds of people," says Mischelle Townsend, the registrar of Riverside County, California. "The first is focused on making sure everything is geared to increasing turnout and making sure no one in disenfranchised. The other is more interested in making sure things get done right, are secure and the law is followed." She vividly recalls the clash between the competing visions of elections during the 2003 recall that put Arnold Schwarzenegger in office as governor of California. The ACLU, the NAACP and other liberal groups convinced a three-judge panel of the U.S. Court of Appeals for the Ninth Circuit to cancel the election because six counties still used punch-card ballots, which according to the anti-recall plaintiffs had a higher error rate than other forms of voting. The argument was that some minority voters would thus have been disfranchised. But an eleven-member panel of the Ninth Circuit unanimously rejected that view, contending that postponing a recall election was tantamount to disfranchising all voters.

"You had the two competing views of what elections were all about right there in those two decisions from the Ninth Circuit," says former California secretary of state Bill Jones. "That split is now playing out nationally in the 2004 election."

Polls bear out Mr. Jones' observation. They also reveal that which vision you have says a lot about how you view the election process. In June 2004, Rasmussen Research asked 1,500 likely voters this question: "If there are disputes in elections, which is more likely to be a problem—that people who are not eligible to vote will be allowed to vote or that people who should be allowed to vote will be denied the right to vote?"

The results are fascinating. A total of 41 percent are more worried about people being excluded from the democratic process; while 36 percent worry about people participating who should not. This result is within the poll's margin of error and effectively a statistical tie. The breakdowns are also intriguing. Kerry voters worry more about people not voting by a margin of 62 percent to

19 percent. Bush voters break the other way, worrying about fraudulent voters participating by 59 percent to 18 percent. That's almost a mirror image. And on the "men are from Mars, women are from Venus" front, men lean toward the constrained vision of enforcing the rules by 41 percent to 39 percent, while women embrace the unconstrained vision of encouraging participation by 41 percent to 33 percent.

According to pollster Scott Rasmussen, significantly more Democrats than Republicans today are convinced that elections are not fair. But that is in part the vision of people out of power. "During the Clinton years my surveys showed more Democrats thought elections were fair to voters, while Republicans were less convinced," he says. "I guess attitudes depend in part on whether your side won or not."

Regardless of how the views of some might shift, whoever holds extreme versions of either vision isn't helping our election system. An excessively cramped view that rules and procedures must be interpreted in such a way as to guarantee that absolutely no improper vote is cast can be regarded as unfairly denying some people the right to vote. Antifraud efforts that cross the line, such as stationing off-duty policemen at polling places as some Republican campaigns did in the 1980s, invite a response such as that of Steven Hill, a senior analyst for the Center for Voting and Democracy: "There must be something about certain types of American voters that Republicans don't trust."

At the other extreme, a loose and lax approach toward the law can lead to unacceptable attempts to game the system such as the one that created thousands of suspect voter registrations during South Dakota's photo-finish Senate race in 2002. Maka Duta, the woman at the heart of that scandal, admitted duplicating signatures on both registration forms and applications for absentee ballots. But she asked for understanding: "If I erred in doing so, I pray that Attorney General Barnett will agree with me that I erred on the side of angels," she wrote in a written statement. In other words, doing the devil's work of forging voter signatures is somehow understandable given her angelic goal of increasing voter turnout.

Despite the passionate opinions on each side as to what undermines the electoral process, there are potential points of agreement that both "visions" should be able to see with equal clarity. Donna Brazile, who served as Al Gore's campaign manager and shares his outrage over the 2000 Florida outcome, nonetheless says, "Both parties should want every voter having information and training to cast a ballot that counts. And if that's done, both parties should support steps to ensure every vote cast is a valid and proper one."

Katherine Harris, the Florida secretary of state in 2000, also endorses having both government and political parties do more to make sure that voters understand how to vote and what is involved. Both women agree that high school curricula, which now often teach students what to eat, how to balance a checkbook and other mundane tasks, should also include instruction on voting. Indeed, many high schools invite seniors to volunteer to work at polling places on Election Day. They earn academic credit in their civics classes as well as a small stipend for the day's work.

Still, everyone knows it will be some time before voter education contributes to a reduction in tension between those who hold so firmly their competing visions of what's important in an election. Meanwhile, we have national elections taking place every two years in an atmosphere of mistrust and bitter division that makes governance increasingly difficult.

The Bloody Eighth

There has been much speculation about when and how the current era of political hard feelings between the two camps—usually described by the catchall term "polarization"—began. Some trace it to the Iran-Contra scandal of 1986; some say the nomination of Robert Bork the next year; some pick the Clarence Thomas fight in 1991 instead. Others say it stemmed from the intense, almost visceral reaction many people had to Bill Clinton, culminating in his 1998 impeachment. Whichever event was most influential, the tone of debate in politics has gradually grown more bitter, personal and cynical over the last two decades.

But the U.S. Congress has never had a more bitterly partisan battle—or one that more plainly displayed the clash of competing visions—than it did in early 1985, when it had to decide the razor-thin election in Indiana's Eighth Congressional District, known locally as "the bloody Eighth" for its many close contests. Voting on Election Day 1984 showed Democratic incumbent Frank McCloskey with a 72-vote victory; a recount by state officials showed Republican Rick McIntyre with a 418-vote lead after several thousand ballots were discounted for technical reasons.

When McIntyre came to Washington to be sworn in as a member of the Ninety-ninth Congress, Democrats had him stand to the side when other members took the oath of office. Then they voted to keep the seat vacant pending an investigation of the contest. The House Administration Committee appointed a three-member task force to oversee a General Accounting Office recount of the ballots, while both men drew a congressional salary but had no job. During the recount, Republicans tried several times to seat McIntyre but were defeated on party-line votes (one of the attempts failed by just one vote when many Democrats were absent). Several weeks later, on another party-line vote, the task force declared McCloskey the winner by just four votes and voted to seat him over loud and bitter GOP protests. Republican members staged a walkout after the House vote.

The subject remains a sensitive one with many House members even today. "It was the event that stimulated the Republican revolution and breakdown of amicable relations between Republicans and Democrats," says American Conservative Union president David Keene. "Every Republican believes that election was stolen during the recount."

Republican Strong-Arm Moves

Democrats say that Indiana Republicans got their revenge for the McCloskey-McIntyre race a decade later, in 1995. After a recount in a state senate race in Lake County, Indiana, incumbent Democratic state senator Frank Mrvan Jr. was behind Republican Sandra Dempsey by three votes. But election workers at three precincts realized they had misfiled some absentee ballots, most of them from Mrvan neighborhoods.

Indiana law stated that in cases of error by an election official, voter intent should prevail. When the issue came up before the state senate, however, the Republican majority ruled that the ballots had been "tainted" and could not be counted. The Republicans booted

Democrat Mrvan from office and swore in Dempsey. The conservative *Indianapolis News* called the move "pure, unadulterated, self-serving partisanship." But Mrvan had the last laugh, coming back to reclaim his seat by defeating Dempsey two years later.

Despite strong-arm moves like that, many Republicans are convinced that their party has a monopoly on virtue when it comes to the devious art of election theft. Anyone who spent time in the 1990s around nicotine-stained GOP party hacks in Nassau County, where lucrative patronage jobs were considered a form of gold and winning elections an easy way to mine for such jobs, would laugh at such a suggestion.

Republicans have certainly at times stepped over the line in trying to root out voter fraud in minority communities. In 1990, the North Carolina Republican Party mailed postcards to hundreds of thousands of black voters telling them they would go to prison if they voted improperly. In 1988, California Republicans in one assembly district hired "poll guards" to carry signs in Spanish and English that read: "Noncitizens can't vote." Four years later, Democrats responded in kind by launching an "election watch" program to prevent any intimidation of newly registered minority voters.

But the most well-publicized incident involving what Democrats claimed was an effort to suppress minority turnout occurred in 1986 when the Republican National Committee agreed to end a ballot security program in Louisiana. It had sent letters to voters in precincts where Republicans had gotten less than 20 percent of the vote in the 1984 election to see if they actually lived at the address shown on their registration. If the letters were returned by the post office—as 31,000 were—the names were handed over to voter registrars with a request that they be purged. A judge found that the precincts where GOP support was below 20 percent coincided almost exactly with precincts where blacks were a clear majority. He ruled that the program had singled out minorities. Democrats sued in federal court and during pretrial discovery found an e-mail sent before the 1986 election by Kris Wolfe, Midwest director for the Republican National Committee, to the GOP's southern political director. The key passage read: "I would guess that this program will eliminate at least 60–80,000 folks from the rolls. If it's a close race, which I'm assuming it is, this could keep the black vote down considerably." Clearly, Republicans had erred by not sending letters to all households in the state when they sought to prune the voter rolls. They agreed not to conduct such programs in the future.

Since then the national GOP has been terminally gun-shy about launching any program that might be characterized as trying to prevent minorities from voting; but the perception that they are doing so lingers. Charges by the U.S. Commission on Civil Rights that massive intimidation took place in Florida in 2000 have proved baseless, but the idea of African American disfranchisement has taken on a life of its own. And Democrats frequently make hay by charging that Republicans are bringing back the ghost of Jim Crow to block minority voting. In her 2000 Senate race, Hillary Rodham Clinton ended her campaign by addressing a Brooklyn College rally filled with Haitian Americans, and told them of a GOP "plot" to place off-duty cops and prison guards at targeted polling places to intimidate voters. "I urge you to be vigilant," she shouted. All that was missing was a reference to "the vast vote-suppression conspiracy." No evidence of such a program was ever found.

Yet some Republican dirty tricks are the real thing. In June 2004 the Justice Department threw the book at the former president of a Virginia-based telemarketing firm who tried to jam Democratic get-out-the-vote phone lines in the 2002 election. Allen Raymond was convicted of taking $15,600 from the New Hampshire Republican Party for get-out-the-vote calls for its candidates and instead using $2,500 of the money to hire another company to repeatedly call five get-out-the-vote phone lines at Democratic offices in New Hampshire. He admitted that his goal was to block the phone lines throughout Election Day. Democrats insist that Mr. Raymond must have had accomplices in the state party.

According to University of Virginia political scientist Larry Sabato, election fraud tends to be "class-based" because "a poor person has more incentive to sell his vote than an upper class suburbanite"; but election fraud is not unknown in the GOP either. The most amusing recent example occurred in wild and wooly Las Vegas, the fastest-growing city in America. In April 2003, Gary and Pamela Horrocks were indicted on charges that they had asked several people who patronized the tavern they owned to fill out bogus voter registration cards and requests for absentee ballots. The year before, Gary Horrocks had been an unsuccessful GOP candidate for the state assembly, losing in the primary to 25-year-old newcomer Francis Allen. Horrocks had contempt for Allen and proceeded to announce publicly that he would submarine her general election race against Democrat Marcus Conklin.

But no one expected him to go as far as he did, or to boast about it. On election night 2002, just after it had become clear that Francis Allen had lost the race by 134 votes, Horrocks showed up at an election party held at Caesars Palace and walked up to Frances Deane, the elected county recorder. "He related to me that he had obtained over a hundred votes in the election for me," Deane recalls. When she asked him how he knew this, he revealed that he had absentee ballots mailed to himself and his wife and they filled them out; he therefore knew how many votes he was responsible for. Indeed, he told her that he was late to the event that night because he had just delivered three votes. Deane still shakes her head at how he was caught only through his own stupidity: "He was so proud. He was like the cat that ate the canary. He was happy with what he'd done."

Horrocks was less happy when investigators fanned out and discovered that 160 voters had illegally registered to vote in the race that Allen lost and had their absentee ballots mailed either to Horrocks' tavern or to the mailbox of the Nevada Association of Concerned Motorcyclists. Horrocks claimed he had been misunderstood. The prosecutors responded that he had been heard perfectly and the evidence they had uncovered backed up his boast. At last word, Horrocks was negotiating with them on a plea agreement. While bizarre, this event wasn't unique, says the *Las Vegas Review-Journal*, but rather a "glimpse at Southern Nevada's seamy underbelly."

Indeed, in July 2004, Las Vegas papers were again filled with stories on election fraud. Larry Lomax, Clark County's top election official, announced that Nevada's battleground status in the presidential race had prompted a surge in phony voter registrations. "We've never seen anything close to this," he said, reporting that his staff had found several hundred suspicious forms. Lomax believed that many more of the five thousand registrations flooding his office every week were also fraudulent but had escaped detection.

"There are stupid criminals out there, and there are smart ones," Lomax said. "We can spot the stupid ones because they submit them in a stack." Lomax added that he wasn't sure whether one or both parties stood to gain from the scam, but the practice of paying people for each registration they turned in rather than by the hour was "incentivizing fraud."

Democrats' Motor Voters

Perhaps no piece of legislation in the last generation better captures the "incentivizing" of fraud and the clash of conflicting visions about the priorities of our election system than the 1993 National Voter Registration Act, commonly known as the "Motor Voter Law."

Observers always regarded the timing behind the push for Motor Voter as curious. It was the first major legislative priority for the new Clinton administration, even though it had just won an election in which the country had seen the largest increase in voter turnout in a generation. Nonetheless, the Clinton White House declared a "crisis" in civic participation and proceeded to ram the Motor Voter Law through Congress.

The act imposed an unfunded mandate on the states by requiring that anyone entering a government office to renew a driver's license or apply for welfare or unemployment compensation would be offered the chance to register on the spot to vote. Examiners were under orders not to ask anyone for identification or proof of citizenship. States also had to permit mail-in voter registrations, which allowed anyone to register without any personal contact with a registrar or election official. Finally, states were limited in pruning "deadwood"—people who had died, moved or been convicted of crimes—from their rolls. Now, people who didn't vote would be kept on the registration rolls for at least eight years before anyone could remove them.

Since its implementation, Motor Voter has worked in one sense: it has fueled an explosion of phantom voters. Between 1994 and 1998, nearly 26 million names were added to the voter rolls nationwide, almost a 20 percent increase. Ironically, as the bipartisan polling team of Ed Goeas and Celinda Lake points out, perhaps only 5 percent of those who register when they get a driver's license routinely vote, which artificially drives down the percentage of voter turnout and leads to yet more cries that something be done about the "turnout crisis."

Curtis Gans, director of the Committee for the Study of the American Electorate, supports some form of national voter registration, but says voter lists from around the country "are virtually unusable" and "more inaccurate than they have ever been." Gans believes that the deadwood clogging our voter rolls provides the unscrupulous with opportunities to vote in the name of someone whom they can safely predict will not show up at the polls to challenge them. This assumption is supported by a 2000 investigation by Bill Theobald of the *Indianapolis Star*, which found that "hundreds of thousands of names, as many as one in five statewide," on Indiana's voter registration rolls "are bogus since the people behind those names have moved, died or gone to prison." Mark Kruzan, the Democratic majority floor leader in the Indiana House at the time, said, "It has become almost ridiculous. I don't know if there is fraud, but it invites the possibility of fraud." Kruzan tried to pass a law to purge the rolls of invalid names, but in vain.

Some registration scandals have been comic. In Broward County, Florida, for example, an eight-year-old girl successfully registered to vote. The error would not have been caught if the girl hadn't been called for jury duty, whereupon her mother called the election supervisor to report the mistake. More improbably, an elephant at the San Diego zoo was successfully registered to vote. Less amusing is the accumulating evidence that Motor Voter has been registering illegal aliens, since anyone who receives a government benefit may also register to vote with no questions asked. An INS investigation in 1996 into alleged Motor Voter fraud in California's Forty-sixth Congressional District revealed that "4,023 illegal voters possibly cast ballots in the disputed election between Republican Robert Dornan and Democrat Loretta Sanchez." Representative Dornan lost that election by fewer than 1,000 votes.

But cries for reform have been countered when the inevitable "race card" is turned up. In 1998, when House Republicans proposed to verify the citizenship of potential registrants, Representative Luis V. Gutierrez of Illinois accused them of "creating unwarranted fear of the Hispanic community in the eyes of our fellow Americans." House Speaker Newt Gingrich responded by saying, "How can we cancel out an American citizen with a noncitizen and not feel that we are somehow cheating the essence of freedom in America? This bill is about citizenship. It is about citizens being allowed to vote."

The lax standards for registration encouraged by the Motor Voter Law have left the voter rolls in a shambles in many states. As the bitter litigation and controversy about recent elections in Florida, St. Louis and South Dakota have shown, the uncertainty surrounding the rolls breeds mistrust and can call the integrity of the whole system into question. Motor Voter has led to "the appearance of corruption" that has, fairly or not, done real damage to American government. In addition, the artificial inflation of the registration rolls has also clearly misled Americans about the state of their democracy by giving a false measure of voting turnout as a proportion of registered voters. Rather than a decline, we may have seen an *increase* in voting as a percentage of legitimately registered voters; but because of Motor Voter, we just don't know.

"Florida's Number Three industry, behind tourism and skin cancer, is voter fraud."
—Columnist Dave Barry

CHAPTER TWO

The Myth of the Stolen Election

The current toxic political atmosphere, in which one side is concerned about voter fraud and the other about voter disfranchisement, is largely the product of the elephant in the parlor left over from the 2000 election. Of course, I'm talking about the Florida recount, the gold standard for botched elections, and all the bitter recriminations it launched.

The Florida battle returned to the news as the 2004 election approached in Michael Moore's hit film *Fahrenheit 9/11*, which begins with a malicious account of what happened in 2000. In essence, Moore claims that George W. Bush, aided by Florida's Republican secretary of state Katherine Harris and the FOX News Channel, stole the election—and that everyone knows it.

There are many issues to debate and argue about the sordid Florida experience, but one of the most intriguing is how a cottage industry has sprung up among liberals to perpetuate this myth. (Jesse Jackson still refers to Florida as "the scene of the crime" where "we were disenfranchised. Our birthright stolen.") As the 2004 election grew closer, the distortions spread beyond Moore's fantasy to the presidential campaign itself. Senator John Kerry told crowds that "we know thousands of people were denied the right to vote." His running mate, former trial lawyer John Edwards, ended speeches with a closing argument about "an incredible miscarriage of justice" in Florida.

Such assertions are simply not supported by the facts. Moore alleges that "under every scenario Gore would have won" Florida without the intervention by the U.S. Supreme Court. But in fact, every single recount of the votes in Florida determined that George W. Bush had won the state's twenty-five electoral votes and therefore the presidency. This includes a manual recount of votes in largely Democratic counties by a consortium of news organizations, among them the *Wall Street Journal*, CNN, the *Boston Globe* and the *Los Angeles Times*. As the *New York Times* reported on November 21, 2001, "A comprehensive review of the uncounted Florida ballots from last year's presidential election reveals that George W. Bush would have won even if the United States Supreme Court had allowed the statewide manual recount of the votes that the Florida Supreme Court had ordered to go forward." The *USA Today* recount team concluded: "Who would have won if Al Gore had gotten manual counts he requested in four counties? Answer: George W. Bush."

Why do liberals persist in propagating the Myth of the Stolen Election? Many of them sincerely believe in it, all this evidence notwithstanding. Others see it as a rallying cry that can bring out the Democratic Party's core voters this fall in righteous anger. The Florida controversy also offers a pretext for some to talk about other changes they want to make in election laws. (The NAACP, for example, wants to "re-enfranchise" four million felons who have lost the right to vote because of their crimes.) Some liberals would even like to extend voting privileges to noncitizens. In July 2004, the San Francisco Board of Supervisors voted to give noncitizens, legal or illegal, the right to vote in local school board elections. The ACLU once sued the U.S. attorney in San Francisco because he matched voting records against lists of legal immigrants who were not yet citizens. The ACLU argued that trying to determine whether noncitizens were voting would have a "chilling effect" on Hispanic voting.

The GOP establishment has decided not to counter the Democrats' allegations of election theft but to urge everyone to move on. "People want their leaders to talk about the future," GOP strategist Ralph Reed told the Associated Press. "They don't want anger and pessimism and personal attacks." Other Republican leaders say the best way to deal with issues lingering from the Florida recount is to ignore them.

But other party members say that Republicans can't simply let Michael Moore-style claims about the Florida recount go unchallenged. "I've had discussions with a number of friends and they say they're tired of repeating the same thing over and over," said Peter Kirsanow, a Republican member of the U.S. Commission on Civil Rights, to journalist John Berlau. "But that's what liberals do and that's why they're successful. They spread these myths until they're accepted as truth. Any sort of falsehood that drives people to vote one way needs to be corrected."

Kirsanow says that the myths must be corrected because "these toxic claims join a host of other pernicious urban legends that filter through the black electorate each election cycle, such as the perennial claim that the Voting Rights Act is about to expire." He is disappointed but not surprised that "those who once obsessed over the incendiary effects of the Willie Horton ad don't seem equally concerned about politicians who traffic in tales of massive disenfranchisement on a third-world scale."

After all the media recounts of 2001 showed that George W. Bush would still have won under any fair standard, Democratic activists have narrowed their charges to the purported disfranchisement of black voters. The Civil Rights Commission, led by Democrat Mary Frances Berry—with only two Republican commissioners at the time—issued a scathing majority report in 2001 alleging "widespread voter disenfranchisement" and accusing Katherine Harris and Jeb Bush of "failing to fulfill their duties in a manner that would prevent this disenfranchisement."

But when it comes to actual evidence of racial bias, the report draws inferences that are not supported by any data and ignores facts that challenge its conclusions. Since we have a secret ballot in America, we do not know the race of the 180,000 voters (2.9 percent of the total number of ballots cast in Florida) whose ballots had no valid vote for president. Machine error cannot be the cause of discrimination, since the machine doesn't know the race of the voter either, and in any case accounts for about one error in 250,000 votes cast. (And, as some have asked, is it not racist in the first place to assume that those who spoil ballots are necessarily minority voters?)

One-third of the supposedly disfranchised voters' ballots were "undervotes"—that is, ballots that showed no vote for president. Think a moment of your own experience as a voter: have you declined to vote for some office on the ballot when you went to the polls? Studies show that over 70 percent of undervotes—where no candidate is selected—are cast deliberately by voters who prefer not to choose from the available options.

The report also discusses "overvoting," the marking of more than one candidate for an office. Even Civil Rights Commission chairman Mary Frances Berry admitted that she had sometimes "overvoted intentionally." In any case, voter error, whether intentional or inadvertent, is not the same thing as racial discrimination.

Nor, as a powerful dissenting report from commissioners Abigail Thernstrom and Russell Redenbaugh pointed out, was the commission able to come up with "a consistent, statistically significant relationship between the share of voters who were African-American and the ballot spoilage rate." John Lott, an economist and statistician from the Yale Law School now with the American Enterprise Institute, studied spoilage rates in Florida by county in the 1992, 1996 and 2000 presidential elections and compared them with demographic changes in county populations. He concluded that "the percent of voters in different race or ethnic categories is never statistically related to ballot spoilage."

Lott found that among the 25 Florida counties with the greatest rate of vote spoilage, 24 had Democratic election officers in charge of counting the votes. He concluded that "having Democratic officials in charge [of county elections] increases ballot spoilage rates significantly, but the effect is stronger when that official is an African-American." Commissioner Abigail Thernstrom argued that "it is very difficult to see any political motive that would lead Democratic local officials to try to keep the most faithful members of their party from the polls and to somehow spoil the ballots of those who did make it into the voting booth."

Finally, despite all the talk about black voters, what about potential disfranchisement of Latinos? After all, there are 2.7 million Hispanics in Florida (compared with 2.3 million blacks), yet in its zeal to politicize the black issue the commission undertook no serious analysis of Hispanic voting. It asks us to believe that nonblack Florida voters (which includes most Hispanics) had a spoilage rate of 1.6 percent compared with 14.4 percent for blacks. Not only is such a statistical disparity not proven, but the academic who did the statistical work for the commission, Allan Lichtman, refuses to make public his data or regression tables.

In fact, Florida 2000 was not a startling anomaly. Ballot-spoilage rates across the country range between 2 and 3 percent of total ballots cast. Florida's rate in 2000 was 3 percent. In 1996 it was 2.5 percent. Glitches occur in every election—which is not to downplay the problem, but to put it into perspective. For example, the number of ruined ballots in Chicago alone was 125,000, compared with 174,000 for the entire state of Florida. Several states experienced voting problems remarkably similar to those in Florida. But the closeness of the 2000 election in Florida made the state a prime opportunity for racial demagoguery.

Doubtful Disfranchisement

Absent from the Civil Rights Commission report are data from both the U.S. Department of Education and the National Assessment of Educational Progress showing that ballot-spoilage rates might be related to disparities in education and literacy. Instead, the report focuses on issues such as the state's decision to keep a list of felons who, according to Florida law, would be barred from voting. It claims that this decision "has a disparate impact on African-Americans" since a higher proportion of blacks are convicted of felonies. That's true, but it is not a voter-discrimination issue, it is an issue for the criminal justice system and the state legislature.

It is also true that the database of the names of felons set up for the state by Database Technologies, a private company, contained some errors. But the liberal-leaning *Palm Beach Post* found that "a review of state records, internal e-mails of [Database Technologies] employees and testimony before the civil rights commission and an elections task force showed no evidence that minorities were specifically targeted." Indeed, the application of the law against felon voting in 2000 skewed somewhat the opposite way: whites were actually the most likely to be erroneously excluded from voter rolls. The error rate was 9.9 percent for whites, 8.7 percent for Hispanics, and only 5.1 percent for African Americans.

Furthermore, the list wasn't created by Katherine Harris or any other Republican. A mandate for the list was passed into law in 1998, sponsored by two Democratic legislators and signed by a Democratic governor, Lawton Chiles, Jeb Bush's predecessor. The law was passed in response to the 1997 Miami mayoral election that was overturned by a court due to widespread fraud, with votes from disqualified felons and dead people. And Harris had no power to remove voters from the rolls. In Florida's decentralized election system, that is reserved for elected county supervisors of elections. The list merely served as a tool for them to use and verify with their own records.

Both the *Miami Herald* and the *Palm Beach Post* found that, if anything, county officials were too permissive in whom they allowed to vote, and this largely benefited Al Gore. An analysis by the *Post* found that 5,600 people whose names matched the names of convicted felons who should have been disqualified were permitted to cast their ballots. "These illegal voters almost certainly influenced the down-to-the-wire presidential election," the *Post* reported. "It's likely they benefited Democratic candidate Al Gore: Of the likely felons identified by the Post, 68 percent were registered Democrats."

Furthermore, the *Post* found no more than 108 "law-abiding" citizens of all races who "were purged from the voter rolls as suspected criminals, only to be cleared after the election." In fact, during all the various lawsuits against Florida, only two people testified they weren't allowed to vote because their names were mistakenly on the list. But in contrast to this trivial number, Bill Sammon, White House correspondent for the *Washington Times*, points out that some 1,420 military ballots, many clearly received on or before Election Day, were disqualified at the behest of Democratic lawyers because they didn't technically comply with Florida's law requiring a foreign postmark. Sammon writes that this and the illegal votes from felons are "what-ifs" that "a truly fair and objective press" would discuss, but the establishment media does not because "they would only serve to reaffirm the legitimacy of Bush's victory."

Other charges from Democratic activists turned out to be "falsehoods and exaggerations." For instance, when the commission investigated the charge that a police traffic checkpoint near a polling place had intimidated black voters, it turned out that the checkpoint operated for ninety minutes at a location two miles from the poll and not even on the same road. And of the sixteen people given citations, twelve were white.

In the end, Florida attorney general Bob Butterworth—a Democrat—testified that of the 2,600 complaints he received on Election Day, only three were about racial discrimination. The League of Women Voters representative testified that it had not received "any evidence of race-based problems."

Time Zone Turnout

Fahrenheit 9/11 also tried to demonize the FOX News Channel, claiming that because a cousin of George W. Bush, John Ellis, was working on the network's election desk that night, FOX gave the public the mistaken impression that Bush had won. The film shows CBS and CNN calling Florida for Gore, followed by a voiceover sneering, "Then something called the FOX News Channel called the election in favor of the other guy." But Moore leaves out the fact that FOX first called Florida for Gore—and didn't call it back until 2:16 A.M. Indeed, all the networks, FOX included, helped Gore by prematurely calling the Florida polls as closed at 7:00 P.M. Eastern Time when in fact they were still open until 8:00 in the state's western Panhandle (which is heavily Republican), and almost immediately they declared Democrat Bill Nelson the winner of the state's U.S. Senate race. (CBS alone declared Florida's polls closed thirty-three times between 7:00 and 8:00 P.M..) Then, at 7:48, the networks, led by NBC, started calling the state for Gore while voters in the Panhandle still had twelve minutes to get to the polls. Of the thousands of prospective voters who were standing in line or en route and heard the news on radio, many gave up and went home.

"By prematurely declaring Gore the winner shortly before the polls had closed in Florida's conservative western Panhandle, the media ended up suppressing the Republican vote," concluded John Lott of the American Enterprise Institute. John McLaughlin & Associates, a Republican polling firm based in Virginia, pegged the loss at 11,500 votes. Its poll, conducted November 15 and 16, showed that the misinformation about poll hours and the premature calling of Florida for Gore dissuaded 28,050 voters from casting ballots; 64 percent of these would have voted for Bush. Even a study commissioned by Democratic strategist Bob Beckel concluded that Bush suffered a net loss of up to 8,000 votes in the western Panhandle as a result of confusion sown by the networks.

While some caution should be brought to these polls since they were taken after the turnout in the Panhandle had become an issue and responses might reflect the political views of those surveyed, statistical evidence on voter participation rates implies a similar drop in voting. In an article in the academic journal *Public Choice*, Lott examined voter turnout rates for Florida counties from 1976 to 2000 and found a significant drop-off in turnout for the ten western Panhandle counties relative to the rest of the state in 2000. The results suggest a net loss of 30,000 votes for Bush. Other evidence he examined on time-of-day turnout during the 2000 election found that the western Panhandle counties actually experienced a relatively high turnout during the first half of the day, but this dipped at the end of the day to slightly below the rest of the state. These data point to a net loss for Bush of between 7,500 and 10,000 votes.

Evaluating these figures is more than a mathematical exercise. In fact, Gore would have had much less moral authority to contest the Florida results had his margin of defeat been 10,000 votes. As the *Washington Times'* Bill Sammon pointedly observes, "A five-digit margin would have been much more daunting for Mr. Gore to overcome than a three-digit one."

Palm Beach Mystery

Something strange happened in Palm Beach County on election night 2000. No, I'm not referring to the butterfly ballot that we all heard about *ad nauseum*. Nor am I going to discuss the unusually large 3,400 votes cast for Pat Buchanan in Palm Beach, many of them in predominantly Jewish and Democratic precincts, nor the hanging chads and dimples that entered our electoral lexicon as a result of what happened there.

In the confusion and chaos after the 2000 election, an anomaly occurred that many people believe ended up costing George W. Bush thousands of votes in Palm Beach. It appears that as many as 15,000 votes may have been altered and subtracted from the Bush total in Palm Beach County.

Bear with me while I go through some numbers; they are important because they suggest fraud. One former Democratic congressman I spoke with said that "no other conclusion explains the bizarre numbers"; and two law enforcement officers said they received credible reports on election night of tampering with punch-card ballots in Palm Beach, but in the chaos of the post-election period they were not told to follow up.

Palm Beach County has grown more Democratic over the years as the numbers of immigrants and elderly retirees from the Northeast have increased. The county voted for the first President Bush in 1988 but in 2000 it gave Al Gore a huge 62.3 percent of the vote, significantly higher than Bill Clinton's 58 percent in Palm Beach in 1996.

George W. Bush's 152,969 votes in Palm Beach in 2000 was such a weak showing that the losing Republican candidate for the U.S. Senate, Bill McCollum, won both more votes (154,642) and a higher percentage of the vote in Palm Beach than Bush did, even though statewide McCollum lost by 284,000 votes (four percentage points) and Bush, as we know, came out ahead.

But what really got some Republicans and outside observers scratching their heads after the recount chaos subsided was the fact that George W. Bush had also been outpolled by the combined vote of the four Republicans running for Congress in Palm Beach, an even more unusual occurrence. Together, the Republican candidates won 158,211 votes in Palm Beach, edging out Bush's 152,969. By comparison, the total of the four Democratic candidates for Congress reflected the traditional drop-off in votes from the presidency to the U.S. House: the four Democrats won a total of 214,307 votes, considerably less than Al Gore's 269,732 votes.

There were other strange occurrences in Palm Beach on election night. Palm Beach County voters seemed uniquely incapable of understanding and using Votamatic punch-card ballots in such a way as to avoid overvoting, that is, voting for more than one candidate for the same office. Palm Beach produced 19,120 overvotes that night, a 4.4 percent error rate—almost ten times the error rate of 0.4 percent in the rest of Florida, or indeed of *any* other large jurisdiction in the country that used punch-card ballots other than Chicago.

Other counties used Votamatic punch-card systems on election night 2000 and did not have nearly the overvote problem that Palm Beach did. In Harris County (Houston), Texas, where almost a million votes were cast on Votamatic punch-card machines, there were only 6,500 (0.7 percent) overvotes and 14,690 (1.5 percent) undervotes (no votes) for president. San Diego County, California—a county with more seniors, minorities and new immigrants in its population mix than Palm Beach County—had an overvote rate of 0.5 percent. So, one should ask, why such a problem in Palm Beach, where overvoting approached 5 percent?

Only in Palm Beach County did Gore gain 750 votes in the initial post-election recount and Bush almost nothing. In 50 out of 67 Florida counties the total change was less than seven votes, and in 63 out of 67 counties the total change was less than thirty votes either way. Further, in 63 out of 67 counties the changes were somewhat evenly divided between all the candidates, in rough proportion to their original number of votes.

In *every* precinct in Palm Beach where Gore got more votes than there are registered Democrats, Bush received less than 60 percent of the registered Republican votes. In *no* precinct in Palm Beach did Bush win more than 80 percent of the number of registered Republicans overall. Indeed, Palm Beach County had the lowest rate of votes for Bush per registered Republican voter of any county in Florida and was in the lowest 10 percent in the country for counties with party registration.

There was certainly no lack of interest in the presidential race that year; it was expected to be close and Florida was a battleground state. Bush was a popular nominee in his own party. There were equally massive get-out-the-vote efforts by both parties. As shown by the absentee ballot numbers, there was equal interest in the election by both parties in Palm Beach. So why did George Bush do so poorly in Palm Beach relative to everywhere else in the state?

It is likely that some 15,000 Republicans went to the polls and something happened: Either they recoiled in disgust at their party's presidential candidate, or forget to vote for him, or (and this is most likely) had their vote show up as a "double-punch" or over-vote that was later thrown out. Some of the overvotes in Palm Beach County represented Gore voters who had also voted for Buchanan, but the 2003 recollections of some workers who recounted the Palm Beach ballots after Election Day indicated that far more ballots showed votes for both Gore and Bush.

Overvotes—where a ballot shows a vote for more than one candidate for an office—should concern us more than under-votes—where a ballot shows no vote for a particular office. Over-votes are often the result of human error and efforts must be made to reduce the chances that they will be cast. But some overvotes may have a less benign explanation. Punch-card voting is partic-ularly vulnerable to manipulation, especially if the ballots aren't counted at the precinct but instead must be transported by car to a central counting station. I was told by two former law enforce-ment officers and a poll worker that they believe ballot tampering affected some Bush ballots on election night. This fraud took place after the polls had closed and the poll watchers had gone home. Precinct officials improperly reopened the ballot transfer cases, in at least one instance while taking the "scenic" route to the election center where the punch cards would be tabulated. Using a nail, pencil or other sharp device, they would take a ballot and punch out Al Gore's name for president. If the person had voted for Gore, the nail would go through air. But if the person had voted for George Bush or anyone else, the ballot would be invalidated, thereby reducing the vote count for that candidate. I was told by one former law enforcement officer that this was done in at least two heavily Democrat precincts that registered an unusually low number of Bush votes.

Remember that reducing your opponent's vote count is just as effective as adding new ballots for your candidate, and virtu-ally undetectable. In the absence of whistleblowers, the only way to figure out if this kind of tampering has occurred is to examine the overvoted ballots for their two choices, and then examine the preferences further down the ballot. Every Bush ballot would have been double-punched with Gore votes too, and possibly even straight-Republican ballots would have been punched with straight-Democratic holes too. The story could only have been uncovered in a closer examination of those 19,000 overvote ballots in Palm Beach County.

Statistician John Lott and other observers, curious about the Palm Beach overvote numbers, urged the media teams recounting the Florida ballots in the summer of 2001 also to examine the Palm Beach ballots to see if the alleged fraud might have occurred. Possible evidence of fraud could have been detected if many ballots showed that someone voted for both Al Gore and George Bush for president and then consistently voted for Republican candidates for other offices.

Despite appeals from Lott and other parties that the recount team examine the Palm Beach ballots for alleged hanky-panky, they were never examined. "They just couldn't be bothered," said Lott. "A great opportunity was lost."

Of course, such an examination would have been suggestive but hardly conclusive. Democrats would have claimed that the fact that more overvotes existed for Gore simply proved he got more votes than Bush in Palm Beach County. But if many ballots featured: a) a vote for George Bush, b) a vote for Al Gore and c) votes for mostly or all Republican candidates below that, a reasonable suspicion would be that someone had punched out Gore chads to invalidate Bush ballots.

One need only have watched the hand recounts in Broward County to see how brazen some election officials can be. And the zeal of local partisans makes some suspect there was hanky-panky in south Florida in 2000. Palm Beach County was one of the last counties in Florida to release its voting results, and Al Gore's strong showing there reduced Bush's lead from 50,000 votes statewide to less than 1,500 when Palm Beach finally came in well after midnight. It is highly likely that after the polls closed and ballots were collected for counting, people would have known how close the race was and that every vote would indeed count—or not count if something was done to it.

National Democrats, aware of voting irregularities in Palm Beach County, hired a Texas telemarketing firm to make several thousand calls into Palm Beach County on Election Day to urge citizens to declare that they were "confused" by the ballot, and specifically to say they were "confused" between the Gore and Buchanan ballot positions. As many news reports have shown, and as Buchanan has acknowledged, many of the 3,000 votes cast for him in Palm Beach were the result of confusion. But more than 3,000 voters claimed subsequently to have been confused and voted for Buchanan, no doubt prompted by the telemarketing calls.

All this shows that Democrats at the national level were indeed extremely interested in the Palm Beach results *before* the polls closed and the ballots were counted. The calls went out before anyone other than election officials knew how many double-punched ballots existed, or which ballot choices for president were double-punched. If someone locally knew that Palm Beach County's vote would be critical that night for victory and if they knew there was already confusion about overvotes, it is certainly possible that someone might have concluded that some additional creative over-voting wouldn't be detected and couldn't be proven.

Apparently we now will never know what caused the Mystery of the Missing Bush Ballots. But that's history. We do know enough about how much proven fraud or electoral incompetence there is in Florida and other states to pay more rigorous attention to it in the future. If we don't, I have no doubt that in another close election, perhaps as early as November 2004, it will be déjà vu all over again. There will be more ballot snafus and more questions about fraud and we will ask ourselves why we didn't address those potential problems when we had the time to take preventive action.

"The fact that voter fraud is generally not recognized as a serious problem by press, public and law enforcement creates the perfect environment for it to flourish."
—Larry J. Sabato and Glenn R. Simpson in their book *Dirty Little Secrets*

CHAPTER THREE

Voters without Borders

I f there was anything like an election law fad in the United States during the 1990s it was the growth of absentee, early voting and voting-by-mail. In 2000, at least one out of five votes were cast outside of traditional polling places before Election Day. That number could rise to over 30 percent in 2004, according to Norman Ornstein of the American Enterprise Institute, and go much higher in the future as states further liberalize their voting procedures. Some 35 percent of California's votes are now cast absentee. Oregon has abolished all but one polling place per county on Election Day and switched to 100 percent mail-in voting. People in our increasingly mobile and hectic society obviously love this convenience. But perhaps we should listen to what some cautionary voices have to say before we redefine ourselves as a nation of convenience voters and abandon one of the only remaining occasions on which Americans come together as a nation to perform a collective civic duty.

Today, twenty-six states have some form of early voting where voters complete the ballot in person at a county office or other designated polling site before Election Day. Voters in Colorado may vote at the grocery store in the weeks leading up to an election. In Texas, some voting machines are set up at retail stores. The time available to vote by early ballot varies. Thirteen states allow residents to cast ballots 17 to 21 days early. In Wisconsin, "Election

Day" is 30 days long. Maine has the longest voting period, beginning an astonishing *three months* before Election Day.

In addition, twenty states have no-excuse absentee voting, which means that any registered voter for any reason can get an absentee ballot in the mail, vote, and then either mail or hand-deliver the ballot to election authorities. Three of those states — California, Utah and Washington—also allow all voters to apply for permanent absentee status and thus automatically get an absentee ballot in the mail for every election. The remaining thirty states still require a voter to have a reason to vote absentee. Reasons include being absent from the county on Election Day; being disabled or ill; being prohibited by one's religion from voting on the day of the election; having to be at work during the hours the polls are open; being away at school or living overseas; or being engaged in active duty in the military.

In the days when Norman Rockwell used to paint *Saturday Evening Post* covers showing people lining up outside churches and schools to vote, it was thought that we all should vote together, and that absentee voting was somehow shirking a voter's true duty and should only be a last resort. In our era of instant gratification, that notion now seems a bit quaint.

But a common voting time was also dictated by the Constitution. Article II states that "Congress may determine the Time of choosing the Electors, and the Day on which they shall give their votes, which day shall be the same throughout the United States." Congress codified this requirement into law in 1872 when it stipulated that presidential elections should be held on the same day throughout the nation. Courts have nonetheless been understandably reluctant to invalidate state laws that go against this dictate.

In 2000, the Voting Integrity Project challenged Oregon's radical decision to adopt a completely vote-by-mail system, which 57 percent of state voters had approved in an initiative in 1998. VIP lawyer Miller Baker said the law made a mockery of the federal statute because ballots could be returned up to three weeks before Election Day. "Absentee voting for good reason is one thing," he told the court. "But Oregon abolishing voting in person is the difference between the exception to the rule and the exception that swallows the rule." He pointed out that the Oregon system had contributed to the chaos of the 2000 presidential election because final results showing that Al Gore had won the state by fewer than seven thousand votes weren't known for weeks.

But U.S. district judge Ann Aiken disagreed. If the Voting Integrity Project was correct, she ruled, "all state absentee balloting laws would be preempted by federal law." In 2002, a three-judge panel of the U.S. Court of Appeals for the Ninth Circuit affirmed the lower court decision. The judges acknowledged the "considerable force" of VIP's argument, but were convinced that ruling in its favor would endanger absentee balloting for the elderly and the disabled. "How can we not at the same time throw out the absentee ballot baby with the bath water?" asked Judge Ruggero J. Aldisert. The panel upheld the vote-by-mail plan because of a "long history of Congressional tolerance" toward absentee voting, particularly in cases where it improves voter turnout.

In fact, however, early and absentee voting may not have boosted voter turnout. The National Commission on Federal Election Reform concluded after examining a voluminous body of evidence that "unrestricted absentee voting probably has not increased turnout at all." The 2000 election saw only 50.7 percent of eligible voters show up, scarcely more than the 49.1 percent who voted in the ho-hum 1996 race. Moreover, turnout had increased by 1.5 percent in states with liberal absentee voting and by 2.6 percent in states with more restrictions.

Curtis Gans, the director of the Committee for the Study of the American Electorate, says that all the studies "are unequivocal in showing that easy absentee voting decreases voter turnout." This is because "you are diffusing the mobilizing focus away from a single day and having to mobilize voters over a period of time." He compares it to the impact a candidate makes on voters when he spends $1 million over the 21-day interval that many states allow for absentee voting, versus the same amount of money focused on a single Election Day. Gans also notes that the people who are really helped by absentee voting are those who would cast ballots anyway, often "lazy middle-class and upper-middle-class people.'

Voting before the fact should also be cause for concern. Absentee ballots allow voters to cast their votes before they might receive useful information or telling insights into candidates. Ross Perot suffered his famous meltdown on *60 Minutes,* in which he accused Republicans of disrupting his daughter's wedding, only nine days before Election Day in 1992. That same year, independent counsel Lawrence Walsh indicted Caspar Weinberger and other figures in the Iran-Contra scandal only four days before Election Day. The John Huang campaign fundraising scandal accelerated in the days just prior to the 1996 election. (Author Elizabeth Drew quotes Bill Clinton as admitting that the Huang issue prevented the Democrats from regaining control of the House.) *Boston Globe* columnist Jeff Jacoby says that having so many people vote weeks early "is rather like having a judge announce that any juror may vote and go home" when the juror decides he or she has heard enough evidence.

More worrisome is the opportunity that absentee ballots provide to the unscrupulous. In 1998, former congressman Austin Murphy of Pennsylvania, a Democrat, was convicted of absentee ballot fraud in a nursing home, where residents who were not very much aware of their surroundings proved an easy mark. "In this area there's a pattern of nursing-home administrators frequently forging ballots under residents' names," notes Sean Cavanaugh, a former Democratic county supervisor. He says that many nursing home owners rely on regular "bounties" from candidates whom they allow to enter their facilities and harvest votes. (For exposing the scandal, Cavanaugh was disowned by his party and he turned independent.)

The National Commission on Federal Election Reform, a bipartisan group co-chaired by former presidents Ford and Carter, issued a comprehensive report on the trend toward early voting, all-mail elections and relaxed absentee ballot laws in 2001. It argued that these methods do not satisfy five essential criteria for sound and honest elections. They are:

1. Assure the privacy of the secret ballot and protection against coerced voting.
2. Verify that only duly registered voters cast ballots.
3. Safeguard ballots against loss or alteration.
4. Assure their prompt counting.
5. Foster the communal aspect of citizens voting together.

Despite such highbrow criticism, however, analyst Curtis Gans believes the trend to convenience voting will be very hard to reverse without a massive scandal. Mischelle Townsend, the registrar of Riverside County, California, remarks that "our society has changed and the public now demands the kind of convenience in voting they're used to getting now in restaurant meals and buying airline tickets."

No-Excuse Ballots

As entrenched as the trend toward absentee voting may be, we should recognize the increased risk it poses in reduced accountability and greater possibilities for fraud and coercion.

"We don't use guns, tanks and bullets to put political leaders in power," Alabama's Democratic secretary of state Jim Bennett pointed out in 1996. "We simply allow absentee ballot manipulators to undermine and quite possibly corrupt the system." Mr. Bennett changed parties to become a Republican the next year, partly out of disgust with how absentee ballots had been abused in the 1994 election. Alabama's laws at the time made absentee voting very easy, and they proved pivotal in 1994, when four statewide races were decided by fewer than ten thousand votes each. One of them, a key race for chief justice of the state supreme court, wasn't decided for eleven months because election officials insisted on counting two thousand absentee ballots that had not been witnessed. U.S. district judge Alex Howard had to step in and declare that attempts to count the ballots were "abominable under the Constitution." He finally ordered that Republican Perry Hooper Sr. had to be seated, ousting the incumbent justice who had remained in office during the entire dispute.

Since the Motor Voter Law made it illegal for states to check individuals' identification prior to allowing them to register to vote and required states to allow mail-in registration, it is possible for individuals to register under numerous false names with almost no chance of detection. They can then request absentee ballots in order to cast multiple votes. The combination of Motor Voter and no-excuse absentee ballots makes it possible for an individual to register to vote, request an absentee ballot and cast a vote without ever being seen by any election official who could verify the individual's existence.

For this reason, as part of the Help America Vote Act of 2002, Congress mandated that states require anyone who registers by mail after January 1, 2003, to provide some identification when casting a first vote. Because the law is cumbersome and discriminates between voters, it is being challenged in state courts; and it does nothing to prevent illegal votes being cast by the millions of people the law grandfathered onto the voter registration rolls sight unseen. "The law will be very difficult to make work because poll workers will have to treat otherwise identical voters differently based merely on if they are first-timers," says Mischelle Townsend. She supports having *everyone* show photo ID, thereby treating all voters equally and improving ballot security.

The secret ballot that is cast in traditional polling locations is important in two ways: it prevents a voter from being pressured and it guards against vote tampering. Absentee ballots are vulnerable to these problems because they are voted in unmonitored settings without any election official or independent observer to make sure there is no illegal coercion by family members, employers, churches, union leaders, nursing home administrators and others. The ability of political parties, candidates and independent groups to appoint observers who can monitor polling sites and the casting of votes is an important guarantee of the integrity and security of our election process.

No-excuse absentee ballot laws make it easier for campaigns to engage in tactics such as requesting absentee ballots in the names of low-income public housing residents and senior citizens, and then either intimidating them into casting votes or completing their ballots for them. Fraud even has its apologists. Richard Cloward, head of the voter rights group Human Serve, told CBS News, "It's better to have a little bit of fraud then to leave people off the rolls who belong there."

Absentee ballots also facilitate vote buying because buyers do a visual check and ensure that the votes have "stayed bought." Ballots cast in traditional voting locations discourage vote buying because buyers have no way of knowing how a vote was cast.

The lack of those controls brought Chicago-style vote buying north to traditionally "good-government" Wisconsin in 2002. The NBC affiliate in Milwaukee, WTMJ, filmed Democratic campaign workers handing out food and small sums of money to residents at a home for the mentally ill in Kenosha, after which the patients were shepherded into a separate room and given absentee ballots. One of the Democratic operatives fled when she saw the NBC camera.

Wisconsin Common Cause director Jay Heck says the NBC footage showed Democratic workers engaged in "manipulative" behavior with a group that was "clearly developmentally disabled." The center had ordered absentee ballots on behalf of all the residents and then allowed Democratic workers to run a bingo game there. The residents were induced to vote with free refreshments and quarters as bingo prizes. In the end, no one was prosecuted; but Robert Jambois, the Kenosha County district attorney, agreed it was a "good policy question" as to whether the laws against electioneering and intimidation at polling places were being circumvented as more and more absentee ballots were circulated by party workers in nursing homes and places like the Kenosha facility.

Former Democratic congressman Toby Moffett can attest to the last-minute surprises that a flood of absentee votes may bring. In the late 1980s, he won Connecticut's Democratic primary for governor on Election Day, but ended up losing by forty-three votes after absentees were counted. Several of his opponent's supporters were later arrested for absentee ballot fraud, but the news came too late to meet the deadline for asking the courts for a new election.

Fraud in Miami

"The lack of in-person, at-the-polls accountability makes absentee ballots the tool of choice for those inclined to commit voter fraud," says the Florida Department of Law Enforcement in its comprehensive guide to voter fraud. This organization should know. The most eye-opening and sordid absentee voter fraud scandal of modern U.S. history unfolded in Miami during that city's 1997 mayoral race, which in its drama, bizarre characters and seedy back-room maneuvering was the equal of any Elmore Leonard or Carl Hiaasen novel.

Miami has long since supplanted Chicago as the epicenter of the country's most colorful political life. It is the home of former U.S. attorney general Janet Reno, who once served as Miami's state attorney. It also is the home of Kendall Coffey, lead counsel for Al Gore in the 2000 Florida recount and a former U.S. attorney under Bill Clinton. He had to resign as U.S. attorney after an incident at the Lipstik Adult Entertainment club in which, after ordering a $900 bottle of champagne on a credit card, he bit one of the topless hostesses. And before becoming the mayor of Miami, Joe Carollo once challenged the late Cuban American leader Jorge Mas to a duel and he wasn't kidding.

In late 1997, Mayor Carollo found himself in a duel of a different kind, fighting a desperate battle to retain his office against challenger (and former mayor) Xavier Suarez. Carollo won 51 percent of the votes cast at polling places on November 4; but Suarez won 61 percent of the absentees, forcing the contest into a runoff. Three days after the initial election, the Florida Department of Law Enforcement arrested Miguel Amador, a Suarez campaign worker, for trying to buy absentee ballots from an undercover agent.

On November 13, Suarez won the runoff with 53 percent of the vote, powered by an even larger flood of absentee votes. (One out of nine votes were cast absentee.) The next week, he appointed an ally, city commissioner Humberto Hernandez, to investigate whether Amador had been entrapped.

Joe Carollo sued to overturn the election. He presented evidence before circuit court judge Thomas S. Wilson Jr. that hundreds of absentee ballots in the initial election had been forged. In February 1998, a grand jury found massive fraud in absentee ballots cast in the first mayoral race. Judge Wilson began a nonjury trial to examine these findings, and twenty-four witnesses took the Fifth Amendment. The next month, he declared the original November 4 election void and called for a new election in sixty days. But the evidence of fraud was so strong that within days, the state's Third District Court of Appeal had overturned Wilson's ruling, thrown out all 4,740 absentee ballots from the November 4 election and installed Carollo as mayor. This extraordinary intervention came because the judges decided that if they did anything less, "we would be sending out the message that the worst that would happen in the face of voter fraud would be another election." The judges went on to note that "unlike the right to vote, which is assured every citizen by the Constitution, the ability to vote by absentee ballot is a privilege."

The *Miami Herald,* which won a Pulitzer Prize for its series on the fraud surrounding the mayoral race, discovered that much of it resulted from a peculiar Florida law allowing a voter to request that a ballot be sent to his or her address. Party workers could then bring the ballot to the voter, who punched it according to his or her choice, then sealed it in an envelope with both the voter and the party worker signing across the sealed flap. The party worker then delivered the "witnessed" ballot to election officials. The *Herald* discovered that this system resulted in massive abuses. Even though it was a third-degree felony for an ineligible voter to cast a ballot, "in Miami, the law was routinely ignored."

There was good reason to change the law. In the 1997 Miami mayoral race, people who lacked all the basic elements of voter eligibility—citizenship, a residence in the city, a nonfelonious record—were actively recruited to cast absentee ballots for Xavier Suarez, who offered not only $10 a vote but also a free shuttle bus to the Miami-Dade County elections office where they could vote under the supervision of his vote haulers. One party worker delivered ninety ballots himself. Others canvassed nursing homes and mental institutions. Some people who had traveled overseas found out later that they somehow had voted without ever having requested a ballot. One Michael Yip voted, although he had died in 1990.

The most brazen vote harvester was Alberto Rossi, a fiery 92-year-old political boss in Miami's Little Havana. He was charged with voter fraud when investigators found more than one hundred absentee ballots secreted in his home, including one for a dead man. His targets were senior citizens, whose signatures he was adept at forging. Rossi was later found guilty of four counts of felony voter fraud. Because of his age, however, he was sentenced to only two years probation.

City commissioner Hernandez, the ally of Mayor Suarez who was given the task of discrediting the charges of absentee ballot fraud, was ultimately convicted of voter fraud himself based on evidence from a police sergeant's wife. Although she and her husband lived outside the city, the woman had agreed on her own to let a friend of Hernandez switch the couple's voting addresses into the city so they could vote. After she was exposed in a *Miami Herald* story, the woman went to the state police and pleaded to save her husband's job. She agreed to wear a wire and arranged a meeting with Hernandez and his aides. Her taped evidence was the key to his later conviction. On the tape, Hernandez scoffed at the *Herald*'s findings: "[Suarez] won by 3,000 votes and you have what, 36 [suspect votes]? Whoop-de-do." He also dismissed the growing evidence of fraud gathered by the *Herald*, saying he could sway public opinion by accusing the paper of racism and of trying to suppress Hispanic political power. And indeed, that was precisely the line of attack used against the *Herald* in an effort to intimidate the paper from running follow-ups on the fraud story.

After Hernandez was convicted, the judge noted the taped comments that Hernandez had made about employing a cynical racial strategy in justifying the imposition of the maximum one-year sentence. But Hernandez's conviction is an exception. Most vote fixers who employ the charge of racism against those who investigate voter fraud usually win out.

The Case of Bakersfield

Bakersfield is a town of 200,000 people located over the Tehachapi Mountains from Los Angeles. It is the part of California that most resembles Texas. Its oil wells produce more oil annually than all of Oklahoma, and its inhabitants include many descendants of the Dust Bowl Okies who migrated here during the 1930s. Country music is big: Bakersfield is the home of both Buck Owens and Merle Haggard.

In 2002, it was also the site of a fierce struggle for a vacant state assembly district. Local businessman Dean Gardner was pitted against Nicole Parra, a legislative staffer in Sacramento and the daughter of Pete Parra, the powerful chairman of the Kern County Board of Supervisors. Over half the district was located in Kern County, which includes Bakersfield, and that was where the campaign became most bitter and the results most controversial.

On election night, Gardner was leading by 2,500 votes with 93 percent of the precincts reporting. Then the Kern County towns of Arvin, Lamont, Delano and McFarland reported in and Parra took the lead by 266 votes. Convinced there had been shenanigans in the rural parts of Kern County, Gardner authorized a local committee, headed by his friend Alberto Llamas, to investigate who had voted. A questionnaire was sent to 14,000 Democrats who had been registered to vote for the first time since the March primary. People were offered a chance to win a gift certificate if they completed the questionnaire. A total of 1,691 surveys were returned, and the results were startling: 76 people admitted in writing that they were not citizens but had voted and 49 indicated they were not registered at their correct residence. Llamas's group then called an additional 1,117 people for a telephone survey. It found that 223 voters didn't live at the address where they had registered and 69 admitted they had voted twice.

A parallel investigation turned up evidence of absentee ballot fraud. Mary Torres of Bakersfield reported that she had requested an absentee ballot but never got it. She went to the polls on Election Day to vote and was told she had already voted. "I had the feeling the people working the polls had no clue as to what they were doing," she later said. "They handed me a provisional ballot, and I filled it out. I have no idea if it was counted."

Several people who joined the California program that allows people to get an absentee ballot mailed to them automatically in every election faced the same uncertainty. Apparently someone had obtained the list of permanent absentee voters and mailed in a new voter registration card for several of them. None of the information was changed except that the new signature was now an illegible scrawl. Election clerks processed the new registrations and wouldn't normally check the new signature. But when an absentee ballot arrived, the law required that the signature on it be compared with the one on the registration form. If they didn't match, the absentee ballot was set aside and not counted. In theory, counties are supposed to notify voters that their ballot wasn't counted, but in practice the letters are sent out either after the election or not at all. The vote is voided and someone's civil right has been abridged.

Llamas's group collected information on absentee ballot fraud, double voting and noncitizen voting representing 1,318 irregular and possibly illegal votes. The evidence was turned over to Ed Jagels, the local district attorney. After a year-long investigation, his office declined to prosecute anyone. One of the assistant DAs concluded that it was not a crime to vote twice, unless the person had criminal intent. Gardner himself says he was told by Jagels, "I've asked my people not to do anything in this case." When asked why, Jagels replied, "We don't want to do anything to upset [Supervisor] Pete Parra. He's in charge of our budget." (Jagels strongly denies that account and says his office didn't turn up compelling evidence of fraud.)

In March 2004, Pete Parra was ousted as a member of the Kern County Board of Supervisors by Mike Robio, a 26-year-old moderate Democrat who called for new leadership in the Hispanic community. Gardner announced he would run again in 2004 against Assemblywoman Nicole Parra.

Liberals' Second Thoughts

Although most complaints about absentee voting come from Republicans and election officials, increasing numbers of Democrats are also questioning the practice. Melody Rose, a liberal professor at Oregon State University, is a severe critic of that state's 100 percent mail-in ballot law. She says it hasn't raised turnout and doesn't save money because it merely shifts the expense from the state to the voter, who must pay for increasingly expensive postage to deliver the ballot. And she believes that vote-by-mail "brings a perpetual risk of systemic fraud." Ballots can easily be stolen from mailboxes and registered voters who don't vote wouldn't bother to alert election officials if they didn't get one.

Ballot security has been promised by the new law, but it is not always delivered. Rose herself once stopped by a library after hours to deposit her ballot only to find an overflowing bin of ballots in a box in the lobby. She could have taken all of them to her car and done some creative pruning based on where people lived or their gender. And on Election Day 2000, witnesses in Pioneer Square in Portland saw campaign workers offering people ballots from baskets and then saying they would deliver them to vote centers.

As a liberal, Rose also believes that mail-in voting reduces a sense of community. "When we dig our ballot out from the junk-mail and credit-card offers, only to vote while watching the latest rendition of 'Survivor,' we cheapen the process and deprive ourselves of a simple reminder of our collective responsibility," she writes. "True reform needs to increase the perceived importance and relevance of voting, not diminish it."

Boulder, Colorado, a classic university town populated by liberals, experimented with a mail-in ballot in November 2001 and had a debacle. KCNC-TV in Denver reported that thousands of ballots were mailed to incorrect addresses, to residents who had moved away and even to the dead. Clerks also rejected a thousand ballots after they were filled out and sent back by voters. In addition, more than one outraged civil libertarian couldn't understand why many of the ballots were opened improperly, allowing election workers to examine them and know how an individual had voted. Linda Flack, the Boulder County Elections Division manager, apologized for the breach of security and vowed it would not happen again.

Other liberals who are still angry over the 2000 election reject the myriad recount scenarios indicating that George W. Bush would still have won Florida even if there had been a statewide recount. But among their "what if" scenarios, one they haven't thought of shows that Gore could very plausibly have won if some of the new liberalized absentee and early voting laws had *not* been in place in 2000.

On average, in the 2000 election one-fifth of all votes were cast either absentee or in early voting. Analysts agree that Gore had a last-minute surge in support, fueled in part by negative reaction to the news of Bush's 1976 arrest for driving under the influence, which hit five days before Election Day. If more people had cast ballots on Election Day, rather than earlier, Gore would probably be president today. A late Gallup poll indicated that 10 percent of independents were "less likely" to vote for Bush as a result of the DUI, and exit polls showed that 28 percent found the issue very or somewhat important. Karl Rove, Bush's top strategist, later told a symposium that the incident cost his boss the popular vote and at least one state. Luckily for him, the fact that more than half the states either had liberalized absentee voting rules or allowed early voting meant that many voters had already "locked in" their preference before the DUI revelations. There was no way they could change their vote.

It is not even necessary to discuss Florida to ponder what might have been. Tennessee allowed people to vote at government offices starting three weeks before the election. Mr. Gore lost his home state because "he did not pay enough attention to it and was late in making personal appearances and putting up TV ads," notes *U.S. News & World Report*'s Roger Simon. Because a full 36 percent of Tennessee's voters cast their ballots before Election Day, "many of them missed Gore's attempt to win the state."

Democrats might do better to look for ways to reform the voting system that would actually improve elections, instead of just making sure the laws do not advantage Republicans. Ultimately, loose absentee laws make exit polls, which help in get-out-the-vote drives, much less reliable; they alter campaigns in strange ways; and in 2000 they hurt the Democrats more profoundly than the butterfly ballots, hanging chads and other well-remembered epiphenomena of Florida.

No More Norman Rockwell

In addition to trivializing the civic ritual of voting and making fraud easier to commit, absentee voting also increases the costs and difficulty of campaigns. "Candidates now have to maintain a very high profile for the entire period and can't just focus on one day," says Richard Smolka, publisher of a newsletter for election officials. And Celinda Lake, a Democratic pollster, says the surge in early voting has changed everything. "Twenty-five percent of voters used to make up their mind in the last seven days of a campaign, and they were a major focus of our energy," she told the Newhouse News Service this year. "Now we may have 25 percent of the voters casting ballots 30 days out." That forces changes in the timing of advertising, and means more of it.

In close races, a flood of absentee ballots can delay the results of elections for weeks. "Anytime you have more paper ballots outside the polling place involved, the greater the chance of mistakes and delays," says Bill Gardner, the Democratic secretary of state in New Hampshire. In Ohio, a worker at the Lucas County Board of Elections (Toledo) found three hundred completed absentee ballots in a storage room more than a month after the March 2004 primary. At least half had not been counted and they ended up affecting the final results of at least one local election.

Absentee ballots also mean delays in counting even when no mysterious boxes are found weeks after an election. "Washington State has regressed in being able to declare a winner since absentee voting exploded here," says John Carlson, a talk-show host in Seattle. In his state, Democrat Maria Cantwell belatedly won a crucial U.S. Senate race in 2000 by 2,200 votes at a time when control of that body was in doubt. "Can anyone say it was a good thing the country had to wait until December 1 to learn the U.S. Senate would be tied for the next six months?" asks Carlson.

Numerous analysts, from George Will on the right to Norman Ornstein on the left, have decried the transformation of voting into an act of convenience rather than communal pride. Absentee ballots not only dispense with the privacy curtain of the voting booth, but, as Will notes, they "consign to private spaces the supreme moment of public choice. Election Day should be the exhilarating central episode of our civic liturgy."

The states should reconsider allowing all voters such an easy rush to judgment. For if the present trends continue, we will become a nation where half of us vote on Election Day and the other half ... well, whenever.

"The machine never misses a chance to steal a certain number of votes and trample all over the election laws. Most of it goes on in the wards where the voters are lower middle class, black, poor white, or on the bottle."
—The late, legendary newspaper columnist
  Mike Royko

CHAPTER FOUR

Politically Active after Death

St. Louis is known for its Gateway Arch, Anheuser-Busch beer and the magnificent Forest Park. But it has also become infamous for having one of the worst-run election systems in the country, a distinction which is of more than local concern since Missouri is always a hotly contested swing state in presidential and Senate elections.

St. Louis's rancid elections have become a civic black eye and also a source of much rueful local humor. Columnist Steve Hilton suggested that the city make lemonade out of lemons and promote its ballot follies as part of a tourism package:

> Hey, stay for the election. It's when dead people vote, and felons. The kids? They're sure to love Ritzy the Dog, who's proudly registered to vote. Don't miss Circuit Court. That's where you get a ballot after saying "I was sick." See a deceased person who needs more time to vote. St. Louis, where we vote past closing time.

The gallows humor acknowledges the fact that if Florida had not dominated all the headlines after the 2000 election and if Missouri had been a little closer, the nation's attention might have been riveted on St. Louis, where abandoned voting machines, unguarded ballot boxes, confusion over poll closing times, and a suspicious phone-bank message by Jesse Jackson threw the entire city's election into chaos.

On Election Day 2000, Gore-Lieberman campaign lawyers filed a suit swearing under oath that their plaintiff, one Robert Odom, was about to be denied his constitutional right to vote because of the times when the polls would be open. The lawsuit became the basis for circuit judge Evelyn Baker's order that the polls be kept open three hours longer in heavily Democratic St. Louis than in the rest of the state. The Missouri Court of Appeals later overruled her, saying that her order "would only permit voting by persons not entitled to participate"; and in that extra time allotted, the court later concluded, "it is probably impossible to know how many voters were improperly permitted to cast a ballot after the polls should legally have been closed." Senator Kit Bond (R-MO) was exaggerating only slightly when he called Election Day in St. Louis "a major criminal enterprise designed to defraud voters."

The story begins the day before the election of November 7, 2000, when William Lacy Clay, the Democratic candidate for Congress running to succeed his father, the retiring incumbent Bill Clay, attended a Gore-Lieberman rally at the America's Center in St. Louis. In his speech to the crowd, the junior Clay said it was his intention to have the polls held open beyond the legal closing time. The next morning's edition of the *St. Louis Post-Dispatch* quoted him as saying, "If it [getting out the African American vote] requires leaving the polls open a little longer, we're going to get a court order to do it."

The next day, both parties worked hard to bring out their base voters, knowing the state was a crucial battleground in the presidential race. George W. Bush and all the other Republicans on the ballot were in the fights of their lives. The governor of Missouri and Democratic Senate candidate, Mel Carnahan, was killed three weeks before the election but his name remained on the ballot. Carnahan's lame-duck successor promised to appoint the late governor's wife, Jean, if the dead man was elected over incumbent Republican John Ashcroft. In the end, the late governor beat Ashcroft by 49,000 votes, or 51 percent to 49 percent. Meanwhile, in the race for governor, Representative Jim Talent was defeated by Democratic state treasurer Bob Holden by just 21,000 votes, or less than 1 percent. (No one knows exactly how much of a role fraud played in these results, but the Missouri secretary of state later found that 56,000 St. Louis–area voters held multiple voter registrations.)

With all of these races in the balance, the pressure to get more voters to the polls became intense. At 3:20 P.M., the Gore-Lieberman campaign, the Democratic Party and Mr. Clay filed suit. The only party named in the suit that was not a candidate or a campaign organization was an elusive figure named "Robert D. Odom." The suit contended that he had "not been able to vote and fears he will not be able to vote because of long lines at the polling places and machine breakdowns that have lasted for several hours." The lawyers filing the suit swore to its validity and their representations about Mr. Odom when they filed. They also alleged that up to 33,000 registered voters had been put on the city s list of inactive voters, leading to further delays if any of them tried to prove they were eligible to vote.

The case was originally scheduled to be heard by circuit judge Robert Dirker, but the lawyers for Gore-Lieberman used their right to ask for another judge to preside over the case. That would normally have meant another judge in Dirker's division, but instead the case mysteriously ended up in the courtroom of Judge Evelyn Baker, who sat on the juvenile court hearing cases involving miscreant minors.

Not that Judge Baker didn't have some experience with elections. Back in 1989, she had rejected an official request from the St. Louis Board of Elections to delay a primary after eleven inches of snow paralyzed the city. The election went on as scheduled, with abysmal turnout as hundreds of thousands of voters stayed home. But while she had been hardhearted in the past, this time she was filled with concern for those like Mr. Odom who were being prevented from voting. "I feel very strongly that people should be able to exercise their right to vote," she told the *St. Louis Post-Dispatch* in a post-election interview.

Attorneys for the election board pointed out that by law, any eligible voter in line at the polls at the closing time of 7:00 P.M. must be allowed to vote. When the board moved to have the suit dismissed, the lawyers for Gore-Lieberman insisted that Mr. Odom needed relief. "Mr. Odom is here and prepared to testify he was

denied his right to vote based on the allegations in the petition,"
said lawyer Douglas Dowd.

Judge Baker never asked to hear from Odom, which was a
good thing for the Gore-Lieberman lawyers because he couldn't
have been in the courtroom. Kevin Cosh, the director of the St.
Louis Board of Elections, found no person named Robert D. Odom
registered to vote in the city. A Robert Odom had been registered
to vote at 1414 Benton Street, but his registration had been can-
celled after his death in 1999. In St. Louis, however, there is something of a tradition for the dead to remain involved in civic affairs.

At 6:30 P.M., after a cursory hearing weighing Odom's complaint, Judge Baker ordered that the city's polls should remain open
until 10:00 P.M., three hours later than allowed by law. She ordered
the downtown office of the election board to remain open for voting until midnight. According to an affidavit filed by Joshua Hen-
ning, sometime between 6:30 and 7:00 P.M., a prerecorded phone
message from Jesse Jackson was sent out. All over St. Louis, residents picked up their phones and heard:

> This is Reverend Jesse Jackson. Tonight the polls in St. Louis are
> staying open late until 10 P.M. in your neighborhood and until mid-
> night downtown. Until 10 P.M. in your neighborhood and midnight
> downtown, at the Board of Elections. Keep the faith. Vote with a
> passion. Keep hope alive.

A similar, apparently coordinated effort was made by Vice
President Al Gore to encourage voters to go to the polls after the
legal closing hour. KMOX and KDNL radio stations each received
a phone call from Gore between 7:00 and 7:30 P.M. Gore urged the
station hosts to broadcast a message from him encouraging people to vote. Given the limited time between Judge Baker's order
being issued and the Jackson and Gore interventions, it is difficult
not to assume that their roles were arranged well in advance.

Judge Baker's decision was clearly at odds with state law. The
Bush-Cheney campaign filed an emergency appeal and a state
court of appeals quashed Baker's order at 7:45 P.M. The new order
required that polls be closed at 8:15. However, locals report that
voting in some precincts continued until after 10:00 P.M. At 7:00
P.M., judges at 29 of the city s nearly 400 precincts walked away

from their posts, exhausted after a fourteen-hour day, leaving ballot boxes unattended or in the care of a building custodian. The next day, St. Louis police found an abandoned voting machine in a vacant lot in the 3900 block of Olive Boulevard.

The tangle of events raised a host of questions, especially given that on Election Day the Gore-Lieberman campaign also filed an identical lawsuit in Kansas City (this time with a real plaintiff) seeking an extension of voting hours across the state. This suit was badly proofread, however, and in several places it referred to the individual plaintiff as "he/she," as if the sex of the voter allegedly denied the right to vote had not been determined. A Kansas state judge rejected this lawsuit.

Another question that remained unanswered was the identity of the mysterious Robert Odom. In an interview with KMOX radio, Gore-Lieberman attorney Douglas Dowd said, "Mr. Odom was introduced to me, for the first time I ever met him I asked him about whether he was registered, and so on, and he was ambivalent about it. Therefore, I informed him and the other people from the campaign that I could not, and would not, use him in the proceedings. I don't think anybody was trying to trick anybody."

The problems with Dowd's account are: a) he verified the petition listing Mr. Dowd as a plaintiff as being truthful when it was handed in at 3:20 P.M.; b) he informed the court that Odom was present and prepared to testify; c) he never informed the court that he thought Odom was in any way equivocal about being registered; and d) Robert Odom was dead.

Kansas City Star reporter Kit Wager was told by Democrats that the Odom mix-up might have been a typographical error and that the intended plaintiff was really "Robert M. Odom," also known as Mark Odom, a political operative for retiring congressman Bill Clay. But there is one problem with this explanation: Records show that "Mark" Odom voted in the 2–3 P.M. hour that day, before the petition was filed. The information presented about Odom to Judge Baker before she issued her order was clearly false on its face.

In an interview with *Insight* magazine, Douglas Dowd changed his story again. "It really was a misunderstanding," Dowd insisted. "He [Mark Odom] thought he was going to be testifying that he saw all the chaos at the polls, but I thought he was one of the voters who had been turned down."

Dowd says he found out during the hearing that Odom had already voted, so he didn't have him testify. But Dowd never told Baker or the appeals court either that the named plaintiff, Robert D. Odom, did not exist, or that Mark Odom had in fact voted. He asserted, "There was no, in my judgment, legal or moral or ethical duty for me to say, 'Judge, Mr. Odom has voted.'"

Downtown

Douglas Dowd may have been a bit obtuse in his discussion of his mystery client, but he was correct in saying that hundreds of people were denied the right to vote on Election Day. St. Louis election officials kept an "inactive voters list" of people who hadn't voted in at least four years and had not returned cards verifying their addresses. Voters on the list, which ballooned to more than 54,000 names in a city where only 125,230 people voted, had a legal right to cast their ballots, but election officials had to confirm their registration with the Board of Elections downtown. Phone lines there were busy all day, and many people were told they should travel downtown to prove their eligibility before an election judge. After the election, the St. Louis Board of Elections settled a lawsuit by promising to have a copy of the inactive voters list available at every voting precinct and to upgrade its phone service.

But not everyone who went downtown was an eligible voter. There appeared to be an effort to flood the election board with voters regardless of whether they were registered, with buses provided by the Democratic Party standing by at many precincts to ferry voters downtown. The election judges, all of them Democrats, issued close to five hundred orders allowing people to vote and never let Republicans challenge any of them.

Some of the orders were clearly rubberstamped. Judge Michael Calvin let Jean Y. Nelson vote even though the only justification for it was her written statement: "I am late registering due to me were [sic] going through a mental disorder." A Mary Ellis sought and was granted an order when her only reason was: "I Mary Ellis, was a [illegible] felon. I was released on November of

1999. I didn't know that I had to register again to vote." Domon Price was given an order without making any written statement. Judge Janalyn Oberkramber requested a ballot with the explanation: "Missed registration deadline date."

An attorney who was doing business in the St. Louis court building on Election Day submitted an affidavit to the U.S. attorney in which he said he was in Judge Calvin's court on Election Day and looked "through a number of these petitions" from voters appearing before him and "between 75% and 85% of them had in the handwriting of the petitioner reasons which were invalid so far as being allowed to vote." When the judge addressed each petitioner, "there was no inquiry by the judge as to whether they had ever registered, attempted to register or anything of the kind." Later on Election Day, Judge Calvin and other judges moved to the lobby of the Board of Elections, from which they issued more orders to the people waiting in line.

Missouri secretary of state Matt Blunt later found that only 35 of the 1,268 court orders to vote met the legal standard set by Missouri law. Among the excuses given by voters and accepted by election judges were: "I want a Dem. president," "For the democratic party," "I'm a busy lady w/ 7 children" and "Found out about Gore from my mother."

The opera bouffe that transpired downtown surprised few court watchers in St. Louis, who know judges there are notorious for having a flexible attitude toward election laws. James Williams, a cook at Micky's Bar downtown, filed an affidavit stating that on the day before the 2000 election he noticed Judge Baker having lunch. She approached him on her way out to discuss the upcoming election. Mr. Williams told her that because he was now a St. Louis County resident, he couldn't vote in the city of St. Louis. She informed him that if he came to her chambers the next morning she would issue an order allowing him to vote in the city anyway. Several other employees of the bar joined the conversation at that point and told her they couldn't vote because they were convicted felons. She told them they could still vote if they had an order from her allowing them to do so and suggested they also come to her chambers for such an order. Her rationalization was that if they had been registered voters before their convictions but were no longer, they could still vote.

Secretary Blunt's investigation of the 2000 election also detailed how the federal Motor Voter Law was facilitating fraud. He calculated that a total of 247,135 St. Louis residents, dead or alive, were registered to vote, as compared with the city's voting-age population of 258,532. That translated to a whopping 96 percent registration rate, the envy even of places like Pyongyang, where not voting is a capital offense.

The secretary of state also made the following findings:

> Sixty-two (62) federal felons voted in that election along with fifty-two (52) state felons; Sixty-eight (68) people voted twice; Fourteen (14) dead people cast votes; Seventy-nine (79) people registered to vacant lots in the city of St. Louis voted in the election; 45 of the city's election judges were not registered to vote, as they are required to do in order to lawfully hold the position of election judge. 250 addresses [were discovered] that are not identified as apartments from which eight or more individuals are registered to vote. A random sampling of 54 of these locations indicates that 14 might have been used as drop-sites for multiple false voter registrations.

Democrats responded to the report by insisting that their only interest had been to ensure that as many people voted as possible. "I think we need to be leery that in the zeal of some of the individuals who are trying to keep rehashing Election Day that their ultimate goal isn't to stymie turnout in the city of St. Louis," said Jim Grebing, spokesman for the state Democratic Party, when confronted with evidence of fraud. William Lacy Clay, by then the city's congressman, said he supported efforts to clean up the city's election record but he recommended that prosecutors recognize that if they targeted too many African Americans for investigation, their actions would be perceived as discrimination: "I'm concerned that this [investigation] will aggravate racial relations in this city," he warned darkly. The Reverend Earl Nance Jr., a local minister, observed, "People in this community, white and black, read race into everything."

The Strange Case of Ritzy Mekler

The specter of election fraud quickly returned to St. Louis in early 2001, just in time for the mayoral primary. The difference was that this time all the major candidates were both Democratic and black. On the very last day to register to vote for the primary, someone dropped off 3,800 voter registration cards. Most were for alleged voters on two specific streets, most were written with identical handwriting and most were fraudulent.

The brazenness of the fraud was stunning. One of the fraudulent voter registration cards belonged to city alderman Alberto "Red" Villa, who had died ten years earlier. "Our election system in St. Louis is like Fort Knox without locks on it," said alderman James Shrewsbury, whose deceased mother's name was found in the pile of new registrations.

Without a white/black dimension to inject emotional paralysis into the issue, action was swift. As a grand jury was convened, even the liberal *St. Louis Post-Dispatch* editorialized that the city "appears to have a full-blown election scandal," and that in any investigation, Governor Bob Holden must "show he can escape the pull of the Democratic machine" that delivered his narrow victory the previous November. (Governor Holden eventually replaced all four members of the city s election board.)

Senator Kit Bond also won national attention for his complaints about the St. Louis scandal, which he called "a blot on the process at least as bad as anything that happened in Florida." In March 2002 he focused television network news coverage on the issue of voter fraud when he brought photos of Ritzy Mekler, a thirteen-year-old springer spaniel who had been registered to vote in St. Louis for eight years, to the Senate floor. Ritzy's owner, retired teacher Margaret Mekler, suspects that her dog became a registered voter because she and her husband put their phone number under Ritzy's name to avoid having their own names in the phone book. "We got a voting identification card that said she had moved here from California, she was twenty-one and had a Social Security number," Mekler laughed. "My dog is very intelligent but I'm not sure I want her voting on who's going to be the president."

Bond said that Ritzy's registration was no laughing matter. "I have a feeling that whoever wrote Ritzy Mekler on the registration form probably could duplicate that signature each and every time they wanted to vote," he told his Senate colleagues. Senator Chuck Schumer, a New York Democrat, responded dismissively by saying that no law Congress could pass would prevent all dogs from voting.

But Senator Bond's campaign prompted an effort to do something about the situation that had led to absurdity and illegality in St. Louis. The new federal Help America Vote Act, which finally passed in 2002, includes requirements that states set up statewide voter registration systems and ask photo identification of the small number of first-time voters who have registered by mail. That just might prevent someone from signing up Ritzy's relatives in the future.

Back home in St. Louis, prosecutors finally swung into action after the 2001 primary registration confirmed that someone was padding the voter rolls with ghosts and had turned the city into a national laughingstock. Circuit attorney Jennifer Joyce made clear that the days when voter fraud would be merely winked at were over. "I want to send a message that our election system should not be tampered with," she told the *St. Louis Post-Dispatch*. "We invite such acts when we don't hold people accountable."

After a two-and-a-half-year investigation, Joyce finally brought indictments in November 2003 against nine people who worked for Operation Big Vote, a well-known registration program. But other than Nona Montgomery, the local manager of the program, the others were small-fry: temporary, hourly workers hired to register people on street corners and in shopping malls.

Three bigger fish who testified before the grand jury in the case escaped indictment altogether. They were city comptroller Darlene Green; Pearlie Evans, a former district director for now-retired representative Bill Clay; and Keena Carter, the Democratic deputy director for the St. Louis Board of Elections.

Carter escaped Joyce's net because it turned out that board members are allowed to engage in partisan activities at the same time they administer elections. In her political capacity, Carter attended a meeting on February 12, 2001, with Nona Montgomery, the key figure in the fraud. Both Green and Evans were also present.

At that meeting, investigators say, a plan was hatched to destroy copies of the false registration cards in order to prevent them from being traced.

Carter agreed to testify on what went on during the meeting, and in exchange was given immunity from prosecution. A month after the indictments, she was quietly taken off the paid administrative leave the board had placed her on and reinstated to her duties overseeing St. Louis elections. "We discovered no wrongdoing," explained the board's new chairman, Derio Gambaro.

2002 Replay

The 2002 elections involved more close races in Missouri. The Republican candidate for U.S. Senate against Senator Jean Carnahan, the widow of the late governor Mel Carnahan, was former representative Jim Talent, himself the losing GOP candidate for governor against Bob Holden in 2000. Intent on making sure this election was better policed than the last one, he deployed dozens of lawyers and poll watchers in St. Louis to monitor the voting. His point man was Thor Hearne, who had helped conduct an investigation of the 2000 St. Louis vote fiasco.

On election night, Hearne and Jack Bartling, a top aide to Senator Bond, were at Talent headquarters in St. Louis County. All the returns had come in by 10:30 P.M. except for those from the city of St. Louis. Talent was narrowly ahead but Hearne was nervous because of the heavy Democratic vote that traditionally came out of St. Louis. He called Catherine Barondo, a counsel in the secretary of state's office who was at the election board office, to find out what the delay was about. She informed him that the board had run the punch-card ballots through the counting machines once and gotten a figure. But workers had just found some six hundred absentee ballots under the desk of an employee and now had to count those. They would also have to recount the votes they'd already counted so that the new votes could be allocated to the proper precinct. The board wouldn't release any totals from the votes already counted until every vote had been tabulated.

Hearne and Bartling became suspicious, jumped into a car and barreled down the freeway toward downtown. Within fifteen minutes they were at the election board office. "I told them it was fine to count the new votes, it was fine to recount the old votes but they had to give me a preliminary total," Hearne recalls. "The entire state had been counted except for St. Louis and everyone knew how many votes Carnahan had to make up if she was going to win." Fearing a last-minute surge of mystery votes that would push her over the top, he asked for a total-in-progress. He was refused.

"A Democratic lawyer named Shauna Clements was there insisting that no totals could be released," he says. "She seemed to be intimidating the election officials who were standing around largely mute." For about ninety minutes, Hearne and Bartling kept demanding a preliminary total. Finally Rufus Tate, the election board's attorney, stepped forward and agreed to release a tally that excluded only the uncounted absentee votes. "That margin wasn't enough to overcome Talent's lead outside of the city," Mr. Hearne recalls. "Those absentee votes couldn't at that point have made the difference with the other votes publicly reported." Talent ended up winning the Senate seat by 21,000 votes.

Elections in St. Louis were a little less chaotic in 2002 than they were in 2000, but there was reason to worry again as presidential elections approached. In May 2004, state auditor Claire McCaskill, a Democrat, issued a scathing report on the election board's procedures in the primary held the previous month. It found that nearly 10 percent, or 24,000, of the city's voters were "questionable." The report tabulated 4,405 dead people, 2,242 felons, 1,453 people voting from vacant lots and 15,963 also registered somewhere else in Missouri or Illinois. At least 935 of the felons, or some 40 percent, had apparently cast a ballot in a recent election.

McCaskill concluded that the St. Louis Board of Elections is beyond repair. She says it needs "local control and direct accountability" and suggests that control of it be transferred directly to the mayor. Governor Bob Holden, a fellow Democrat, agreed.

In June 2004, another scandal broke when the Associated Press turned up evidence that America Coming Together, an anti-Bush group funded by $5 million from financier George Soros, had hired dozens of felons to go door-to-door and register voters in Missouri, and also in Florida and Ohio, two other battleground states. ACT's counteroffensive was swift and predictable. First, the organization denied that it had employed *violent* felons. Then when the Associated Press reported that ACT employees did indeed include people convicted of assault and sex offenses, the group admitted it might also have hired felons in fourteen other battleground states. It also promised to fire anyone guilty of "violent or other serious offenses." In some cases it won t have to; four felons it hired in Missouri have already been sent back to prison, including one for endangering the welfare of a minor. That's one reason the Missouri Department of Corrections banned ACT from its list of potential employers for parolees in halfway houses. Noting that the felons would have to handle driver's license information and telephone numbers as part of the voter registration process, the department concluded that "from a public safety standpoint, we didn't want offenders to be in a situation where they would be handling that information."

ACT also denied that it is violating federal election laws that prohibit it from engaging in partisan activity on behalf of the Kerry campaign, even though its Web site says it is "laying the groundwork to defeat George W. Bush and elect Democrats." Its roster of staffers is chock full of Democratic operatives with close ties to Mr. Kerry. Just this month, ACT staffer Rodney Shelton left to join the Kerry campaign as its Arkansas state director. At the same time, former Kerry campaign manager Jim Jordan has joined ACT. Federal law forbids any coordination between ACT and the Kerry campaign, but it is impossible to enforce.

Ellen Malcolm, ACT's president, says the attacks on her group represent an attempt "to distort and play politics with this situation, to attempt to disrupt ACT and our grassroots activities." But in light of the felon scandal, ACT's activities now merit closer scrutiny, because they may be making the problem of our sloppy voter rolls worse. The Federal Election Commission found in 2002 that 12 percent of all registered voters nationally were "inactive voters," and thus subject to possible misuse by having someone else vote in their name. In Missouri, a swing state that George W. Bush narrowly won in 2000, ACT bought at least $40,000 worth of voter lists from the state's Democratic Party and then paid 75 canvassers between $8 and $12 an hour to go door-to-door and sign up new voters. Since last year, they have signed up 44,000 new voters in St. Louis alone.

The St. Louis Board of Elections reports that over half of the registrations turned in by ACT are invalid, mostly because they are duplicate registrations for existing voters. But given the board's track record with numbers, it is uncertain how many of the other names may also have question marks attached to them.

Many of those questions may never be answered, because anyone who combats election fraud or questions the accuracy of voter rolls in St. Louis and elsewhere around the country is likely to come in for abuse. When the *Miami Herald* won a Pulitzer Prize for its reporting on the rampant absentee ballot fraud in that city's 1998 mayoral election, the Pulitzer jury referred to "a public campaign accusing the paper of ethnic bias and attempted intimidation." Local officials in several states who have tried to purge voter rolls of felons and noncitizens have been hit with nuisance lawsuits alleging civil rights abuse.

It's no surprise that many voter rolls such as those in St. Louis remain clogged with voter deadwood or that prosecutions for voter fraud are rare and almost always target only small-bore flunkies. All the conditions still exist for voter fraud to occur in St. Louis again this year, and this time federal mandates will require that anyone who shows up wanting to vote must be allowed to cast a provisional ballot. Those who might want to question their validity should expect that somebody will stand up and yell "racist," no matter how crowded the election theater is with irregularities.

"Sometimes I sit here and look out the window
and think, 'Boy, if the city only knew.' "
—Leigh DeMaci, a Dallas assistant district attorney
   who specializes in voter fraud

CHAPTER FIVE

The Ghost of LBJ

ost Democrats downplay the existence of election
fraud, but not Representative Ciro Rodriguez, the
chairman of the Congressional Hispanic Caucus. He's
from Texas, the capital of Stolen Elections. In March
2004 he lost his Democratic primary to former Texas secretary of
state Henry Cuellar in a redrawn district that stretches from the
barrios of San Antonio to the Mexican border at Laredo.

Representative Rodriguez initially had led on election night
by 126 votes, but weeks later a recount of Cuellar strongholds in
Laredo's Webb County and next-door Zapata County gave him
the lead. After another recount, Cuellar was ahead by 58 votes and
certified the winner. Rodriguez promptly challenged the result,
claiming there had been systemic voter fraud. Many observers
agreed with him that southern Texas had a longstanding problem
conducting honest elections. "There are still political bosses and
questionable activities," says Geronimo Rodriguez, who was a
regional director for the Gore-Lieberman campaign in 2000.

The recount in Zapata County even turned up a missing ballot box with 304 uncounted ballots, some 10 percent of the total
cast. Over 80 percent of those went to Cuellar. Officials in Webb
County reported that their recount came up with 115 more votes
than they had first reported. Cuellar won every one of the newly

discovered votes. A second recount of Webb County then reduced Cuellar's vote there by 145 votes.

"It stinks to high heaven, to be honest with you," says John Puder, a top adviser to Ciro Rodriguez. But Doroteo Garza, who oversaw the recount in Zapata, disputes any charges of chicanery. "The boxes were not tampered [with]-everything's there. The seals were not broken. The only thing that we can suspect is that those ballots were there, but they were not counted." Nonetheless, some supporters of Rodriguez see the ghost of Lyndon Johnson striding again across the plains of southern Texas.

Part of Texas electoral legend involves the way Lyndon Johnson saved his political career in 1948 when he was losing a Democratic primary for U.S. Senate. A full week after the primary, an operative for political boss George Parr, "the Duke of Duval County," adjusted the vote total of Ballot Box 13 in Jim Wells County to include 200 additional votes for Johnson. That gave him an 87-vote victory statewide out of over a million cast. But the voters of Box 13 were an orderly bunch: they apparently had cast their ballots in exact alphabetical order. Nevertheless, Johnson's victory survived every legal challenge and set him off on a career path that led to the White House.

The late J. K. Ray, an agent for the state's tax division, joined Texas Ranger Frank Hamer for an investigation of Box 13. When they arrived at a bank in Jim Wells County, the two men found it surrounded by armed *pistoleros*, thugs and other assorted political henchmen committed to an LBJ victory. Brandishing their guns, Hamer and Ray made their way through the crowd and into the building. They discovered men burning ballots and altering the voter rolls. Ray's granddaughter, Kay Daly, recalls, "He always said he witnessed the crux of the scam that permitted sheriff's deputies and election officials to steal the election for LBJ." In 1977, Johnson biographer Robert Caro interviewed Luis Salas, the man in charge of Ballot Box 13, and after three decades of denials got him to admit, "Johnson didn't win that day. We stole it for him."

Old-style ballot-box stuffing isn't as easy in the Lone Star State as it was back then, but there is still enough mischief for Texas to retain its status as a case study in American election fraud. A cottage industry of get-out-the-vote organizers called *politiqueras*, or paid vote brokers, recruit the elderly and disabled to vote by mail. Dispensing advice, they sit nearby while voters mark their ballots in kitchens or living rooms. Often they will leave with the marked ballots, promising to stamp them and mail them for the voter.

"There is a lot of abuse. People complain to me that someone picked up their ballot, and they didn't even vote," says Guadalupe Martinez, the chairman of the Jim Wells Democratic Party. *Politiqueras* often earn hundreds of dollars for their vote harvesting. "A person running for office here ignores them at their peril," says Jerry Polinard, a political scientist at the University of Texas.

Alfonso Casso, a former member of the Laredo City Council, says that the existence of "a one-party system where the literacy rate is low" perpetuates the practice of voters "selling their vote to the highest bidder without any regard or knowledge of the issues."

Herminia Becerra, a 73-year-old grandmother who calls herself the queen of the *politiqueras* in Brownsville, says she is actually working in behalf of the average person, choosing candidates who will help the community. "We are the voice" of the community and "problem solvers," she says. For the most part, criticism of their role comes from an Anglo establishment that used to intimidate poor Hispanics, who only recently have gained some political power. This makes their criticism automatically suspect.

But not everyone who is troubled is Anglo. In March 2004, three *politiqueras* were accused of harassment by elderly voters in Hidalgo County. Teresa Navarro, Hidalgo County's election administrator, ended the practice of letting vote brokers pick up hundreds of applications for mail-in ballots after large numbers of them were turned in with the same post office box listed as the home address. Bruce Sherbet, the election administrator for Dallas County, calls such precautions wise. "If you have voter fraud in an election today, there is a 90 percent chance it's in the mail-in ballot area," he says. "We've tried without success to get legislation to bring more accountability."

Former representative Debra Danburg, a Houston Democrat who served as chairman of the election panel of the Texas House until 2003, says the actions of many vote brokers are "victimizing the elderly.... I wish the older citizens' lobby group would see the fraud I'm seeing and start reacting like victims of fraud." Republicans now have complete control of Texas state government but have been slow to implement reforms. "It's out of fear they will be tagged as racist and preventing elderly people from voting," says Texas GOP representative Ron Paul. But he says many Republicans are mistaken if they think fraud occurred only in Hispanic counties. "There's fraud in the suburbs, but it's done more subtly."

Representative Rodriguez doesn't think much subtlety was involved in his 58-vote defeat. KENS-TV searched a partial list of two dozen suspect voters identified by the Rodriguez team, first matching them against Webb County's voter database, then confirming that they voted and checking their address on file at the elections office. Francisco Garcia of 12 Ventura Street in Laredo was listed as having voted in person March 9, but they couldn't locate his home. A few blocks over, Cristina Vasquez of 319 Water Street was also listed as having voted March 9, although homes on that side of the street had been swept away in a 1998 flood. Elder Murillo confirmed he had voted, but said none of the five other voters listed at his address had lived there for at least five years.

Rodriguez' attorney John Ray said that if the courts had granted his client a hearing, he would have presented evidence of several hundred suspect votes. Rodriguez aides also pointed to the strange recount in Zapata County, where they said the ballots were stored in a bank owned by a Cuellar contributor and guarded by police officers who had relatives who supported Cuellar.

T. J. Connolly, a Cuellar spokesman, notes that in any trial the Cuellar forces could present evidence of shenanigans in San Antonio, where Rodriguez won over 80 percent of the vote and where county officials admit at least forty-two dead people voted. "We had recounts and an election certified," he says. "Mr. Rodriguez can't go trolling until one day he can somehow cobble [together] a theory that allows him to win and then present it to a judge." Indeed, in July 2004 the Texas Fourth Court of Appeals rejected Congressman Rodriguez's request for a trial and his request for a new election.

We will never know exactly what voting irregularities took place in his race, and no one has linked Henry Cuellar to anything improper. But the controversy certainly begs the question why we are still wondering what goes on in Texas elections more than half a century after Ballot Box 13 was discovered. Gilberto Quezada, the author of a book on Texas' tainted history of voter fraud, says "there is a close correlation of events between what is happening now with Ciro and Henry and what happened in 1948 in Zapata." He says that two years ago he gave a copy of his book to Representative Rodriguez. "I said, 'Ciro, be sure and read this.' I don't think he did."

CHAPTER SIX

Election Reservations

E lections in South Dakota are usually polite affairs, conducted with the kind of civility one often finds in rural states. But the 2002 election for U.S. Senate between incumbent Democrat Tim Johnson and his Republican challenger, Representative Jim Thune, was dramatically different. The stakes were high: Democrats had 50 Senate seats going into the election, Republicans had 49, and there was one Democratic-leaning independent. South Dakota's race could determine both which party controlled the Senate and whether Tom Daschle, South Dakota's other senator, would continue as the powerful majority leader.

Both parties poured in outside resources, workers and lawyers. Democrats mounted a massive voter registration drive that signed up 17,000 new voters in a state where fewer than 300,000 votes are cast. The signups drew fire after hundreds of voter registration cards and absentee ballot requests were discovered to have been forged. Two individuals who received payments, directly or indirectly, from the Democratic Party were charged with forgery. A total of 277 South Dakotans told the state Department of Criminal Investigations that their names had been forged on absentee ballot requests and the FBI reported 15 additional forgeries.

Democrats denied approving of any illegal behavior and said Republican complaints about registrations collected on Indian reservations were actually a veiled attempt to discourage Indians from voting. If so, such alleged intimidation failed. On Election Day, turnout on the reservations soared by 10 to 15 percent. But the process left a sour taste in voters' mouths. There were complaints that some polling places in Democratic strongholds were held open for an extra hour, that illegal electioneering occurred in many polling places, that unregistered individuals were allowed to vote and that Democratic lawyers had interfered with the election process. In some counties where over half the people live below the poverty line, there were also allegations that money had changed hands in return for votes.

Election night was a nail-biter, with Thune consistently taking the lead after midnight. At 3:41 A.M., Thune had a 3,729-vote lead with what Clifford Scott, the former chairman of the South Dakota Democratic Party, later called "all the no-reservation counties reporting. But either by accident or design, the majority of the reservation precincts ... had not reported." At 6:38 A.M. on Wednesday, with just six of the state's 844 precincts left to count, Thune led Johnson by 949 votes. When three of those precincts came in, Thune's lead narrowed to 188 votes. The precincts still out were all in Shannon County, home of the giant Pine Ridge Reservation and the Oglala Sioux. When those were counted, Senator Johnson had carried Shannon with 92 percent of the vote and won statewide by 524 votes.

Because he wanted to remain active in state politics, Thune chose not to contest the outcome. But others who did study the results were appalled. Michael New, a postdoctoral fellow at the Harvard-MIT Data Center, analyzed the South Dakota returns and reported a series of startling facts to the *Wall Street Journal*. While Democrat Tim Johnson ran statewide about 12 percentage points behind what Tom Daschle had received in his 1998 Senate victory, in Shannon County he ran about 12 percentage points ahead, getting 92 percent of the vote compared with Daschle's earlier 80 percent. Nowhere else in the state did Johnson improve his vote share relative to Mr. Daschle.

Voter turnout for the 2002 Senate election was up 27 percent statewide compared with 1998, but in Shannon County turnout increased by 89 percent. Again, no other county in the state, including other largely Indian counties, showed comparable turnout increases. Admittedly, Shannon County is heavily Democratic, but Thune got only nine more votes there than Daschle's opponent in 1998, notwithstanding the much larger turnout.

Democrats said that the increase in their vote was attributable to their successful efforts at signing up new voters and getting them to the polls. But Republicans signed up new voters in Indian country, too, and they wonder why only in Shannon County did so few of them show up. In the other three South Dakota counties where Indians constitute more than two-thirds of the population, Mr. Thune gained between 23 percent and 43 percent more votes than the GOP candidate in 1998. As Michael New concedes, "this could all be a coincidence." But "this trifecta of late results, high turnout and unusually strong support for the Democratic nominee should, if nothing else, arouse suspicion."

Suspicion about the 2002 election, stoked by the October scandal over forged voter registration forms, was running high even before Election Day controversies cast a cloud over the results. KELO, a Sioux Falls TV station, reported that a survey of six hundred voters found that 63 percent said "they were somewhat or very concerned voter registration fraud will change the outcome of the election."

Democrats in Indian Country

Democratic efforts to target the 9 percent of South Dakotans who have Indian roots began in the spring of 2002. Terry McAuliffe, the chairman of the Democratic National Committee, told the *Sioux Falls Argus-Leader,* "we're actively going after the Native American community." By September, the Democratic Senatorial Campaign Committee was boasting that the "party has been working closely with the Native population to register voters and Senator Johnson has set up campaign offices on every reservation." After voter fraud problems were reported in early October, however, the Johnson campaign denied it had any offices on the reservations.

According to the Associated Press, "when a reporter called the Lower Brule Reservation, a woman said she was a field officer for Johnson's campaign and referred the reporter to Johnson's office. Johnson campaign manager Steve Hildebrand said that the woman was mistaken and that she worked for the Democratic Party." After a Johnson spokesman denied the existence of any Johnson offices on reservations, Senator Johnson contradicted him by telling the *Washington Times*, "We do have campaign offices in Indian Country."

Later, despite claims by Democrats in May that the Johnson campaign and the Democratic Party were working "hand-in-hand to forward" registration efforts, Senator Johnson told *Newsweek*'s Howard Fineman that voter registration was "the state party's business, not my campaign's."

The *Washington Post* reported, "For months, South Dakota Democrats have suggested that Native American voters might provide just enough votes to help Sen. Tim Johnson win." State Democrats told the *Christian Science Monitor* they expected ten thousand new votes from the Indian reservations that year. Russell LaFountain, the director of Native Vote 2008, said his organizers were encouraging "strong absentee balloting." But by October, the South Dakota Democratic Party was backing away from suggestions that aggressive voter drives on reservations were a key part of their strategy.

Despite last-minute efforts by Democrats to distance themselves from their efforts, the *Chicago Tribune* found the party's footprints all over the reservations. When it covered the opening of the Democratic voter registration office on the Crow Creek Indian Reservation, the paper interviewed one woman who said, "They told us to vote Democrat. We don't vote Republican here.'"

In order to target Native American voters successfully, Democrats decided to pay $3 per-head bounties for voter registration cards and absentee ballot requests, which in poor areas created incentives to commit fraud. The liberal *Sioux Falls Argus-Leader*, which endorsed Senator Johnson for reelection, criticized the practice of paying voter bounties and concluded that "such a system itself leads to fraud."

In Pennington County, where Rapid City is located, six dead people were registered to vote. Lyle Nichols, who "registered" the dead people, gathered his bounties by copying names from the phone book or from obituaries, according to the county sheriff. Nichols was on work release from jail and ironically, 25 percent of the money he earned from the registrations went to the county to cover his room and board costs.

The bounty-hunting system created by the South Dakota Democratic Party resulted in the filing of five counts of forgery against Nichols, although prosecutors could have filed 226 counts of forgery. He had been paid by an organization that had been given $2,500 by the Democratic Party. In July 2003, Nichols pleaded guilty to the lesser charge of possessing a forged instrument in order to avoid jail. Prosecutors dropped five forgery counts, each of which carried a maximum five-year prison term. Nichols told Judge John "Jack" Delaney that he had handed out cards to people he knew in the vicinity of Prairie Market at 11 New York Street. When Delaney asked whether Nichols' helpers were intoxicated as they filled out the cards, Nichols replied, "Oh, yeah. Definitely."

Another case of voter registration fraud involved Becky Red Earth Villeda, also known as Maka Duta, who was paid more than $13,000 in bounties from the Democratic Party before county auditors discovered that she had turned in hundreds of illegal registrations and the Democrats fired her. Maka Duta put out a press release claiming that her work was directly overseen by supervisors at state Democratic headquarters.

As with Nichols, Maka Duta was not the most reliable employee the Democrats could have hired. In 1998, she had been accused of submitting a forged election petition during her campaign for a tribal office on the Flandreau Reservation. She was banned from tribal offices in February 2000. According to state investigators, Maka Duta was linked to as many as 1,750 questionable absentee ballot applications. By her own estimate she filled out 1,000 registration forms. As part of her job, she ensured that prospective voters registered as Democrats. One woman who witnessed Maka Duta signing up voters noted that on the registration card, "Democrat was already written there."

Some of the registrations were indeed creative. Denise Red Horse of Ziebach County died in a car crash on September 3, 2002. But both Ziebach and Dewey counties found separate absentee ballot applications from her dated September 21 in bundles of applications mailed from Democratic headquarters. Maka Duta had bought a county history book that contained many Dewey

County names. Some turned up in the pile of new registrations. Mable Romero says she received a registration card for her three-year-old granddaughter, Ashley. In both Dewey and Ziebach counties, the number of registered voters easily exceeded the number of residents over age eighteen counted by the 2000 census.

The forged registrations were collected by Duta, turned over to Democratic officials and then mailed directly to voter registrars from the party's offices. "All of those counties are being flooded with new voters," Dewey County auditor Adele Enright said at the time. "We just got a huge envelope of 350 absentee ballot applications postmarked from the Sioux Falls office of the Democratic Party."

At first, Democrats insisted that the registrations were valid. "A party official says absentee applications sent to their office by independent contractors get the once-over by party employees," reported KELO on October 16, as the scandal broke. If so, the oversight was spotty. Renee Dross, an election clerk for Shannon County, said her office received some 1,100 new voter registrations in a county with only 10,000 people, and "many were clearly signed by the same person." Some registrants actually lived in neighboring Nebraska. Steve Aberle, the Dewey County state's attorney, said many of the applications were in the same handwriting. When the problems became obvious, Democratic officials said they promptly fired Duta and then told reporters they were the first to bring the fraud to light. Adele Enright, a Democrat, called that claim untrue and "pure spin."

For her part, Maka Duta maintained she had always complied with instructions from the Democratic Party. But she nonetheless tried to cover her tracks when investigators came calling. Attorney General Mark Barnett said she had apparently tried to burn the original applications but then decided to retrieve them. Investigators suspect she tried to copy information from the original forms, including the signatures, onto new applications. "It gets stranger every day," Barnett said. "She claims they are the legitimate signatures [on the charred paper]." Maka Duta soon released a statement admitting that she had duplicated signatures for voters in Dewey and Ziebach counties but denied any wrongdoing, saying all her applications "were submitted to my supervisor at the South Dakota Democrat Party."

Auditor Enright discovered that the 350 absentee ballot applications that Dewey County got from the state Democratic Party all indicated that the signers would be out of the county on Election Day, a remarkable event in a jurisdiction with only 3,500 registered voters. She concluded that "there's no accountability" with the Democratic Party's management of the voter registration program.

The pre-election voting irregularities were so widespread that South Dakota secretary of state Joyce Valentine had to adopt special vote-counting procedures. On October 28, she announced in response to "actions that challenge our election system by introducing fraud" that election workers shouldn't place any absentee ballots in the ballot box until after the polls had closed. This allowed any voter for whom an absentee ballot may have been fraudulently requested to vote in person and have their vote count. "It appears we were able to get (Maka Duta) stopped before she actually cast any fraudulent ballots," said Larry Long, South Dakota's chief deputy attorney general. "But it's conceivable that she was able to get ballots cast that we don't know about."

Some fraudulent absentee ballots may indeed have been counted. In Todd County, on the Rosebud Indian Reservation, Noma Sazama, a Republican election board member, reported a number of ballots in which the votes "all looked like they had been signed by the same person, but the signatures matched what was on file, so they were counted."

Maka Duta was ultimately charged with only nineteen counts of forgery, despite evidence that she had forged at least 277 documents. Tribal officials claimed that the attorney general lacked the power to serve subpoenas on tribal land to collect evidence in several of the cases, and the charges had to be dismissed. Maka Duta was then indicted a second time for eight counts of forgery, but these charges were later dropped altogether when an "expert" (a retired rural sheriff) concluded that there wasn't enough evidence to prove forgery. The individuals involved, of course, had already sworn that their names had been forged. A former lawyer for the Attorney General's Office told me the case had been only reluctantly pursued with minimal resources, and the office was happy to be rid of the case, given the charges of racism that accompanied it.

Intimidation

Democrats quickly resorted to intimidation in order to turn the
voter registration scandal in their favor. They bitterly attacked journalists who reported on it. After Shelley Keohane, a reporter for
KSFY-TV in Sioux Falls, did a report on people who had applied
for absentee ballots without their knowledge, Democrats met with
the station's management and demanded that she and an anchor-
man be fired for bias. The station refused. Later it was learned that
a station employee had been spying for Democratic operatives,
giving them information and documents on the station's plans to
cover the story. He was fired after the election.

Senators Daschle and Johnson toured the South Dakota reservations together just before the election and had staffers distribute flyers entitled "Don't Be Intimidated!!!" They proclaimed:

> The Republican Party doesn't want Native people to vote. They
> know that when we vote, our voice is heard and Republicans lose.
> They have manufactured a handful of allegations and charged "mas-
> sive voter fraud" on the reservations. This is just not true. Our peo-
> ple are proud, and we will not be intimidated.

The flyer concluded, "Empower yourself! Vote Democratic."

Copies of the flyer were found at the polls in Mission and
posted on the door at the St. Thomas Hall polling place on Tuesday. "There's not supposed to be any campaign material in the
building, and I picked one up in the building," reported Noma
Sazama.

In an eye-opening article in *National Review*, Byron York
described how Democrats initiated an extensive voter-hauling operation on Election Day that in some places illegally commandeered
polling places. Ms. Sazama told York that on Election Day her polling
place was filled with Democratic lawyers. They quickly made the
kitchen of St. Thomas Hall their transportation nerve center, coordinating the routes of dozens of vans that had been hired to bring
workers to the polls. "It shouldn't be their right to run their campaign strategy from the polling place," said Ms. Sazama.

Delvin Meyer, a GOP poll watcher, concurred: "The buses
were controlled from the kitchen. As far as I'm concerned, that's

illegal." Nancy Wanless, a Democrat who was the precinct's election supervisor, was also resentful that her polling place had turned into a campaign headquarters, with Democratic lawyers monopolizing the only phone. Her protests were ignored. "I felt like they were trying to intimidate me," she later complained.

Democratic operatives ran similar operations in dozens of other precincts. Each team leader had boxes of index cards, each of which included information about prospective voters. The cards were used to determine which voters had voted and then given to Democratic van drivers, who would seek out voters who had not been to the polls. While the prospective voters were in the Democratic van hauling them to the polls, they were given the flyers charging that "the Republican Party doesn't want Native people to vote." On the reverse side of the flyer were sample ballots with all the Democratic candidates' boxes filled in. Poll watcher Ray Stewart observed that "[p]eople delivered to the polls by the Democratically coordinated van operation carried the 'Don't Be Intimidated' flyers with them as they left the vans." The Democratic vans, in short, were used to instruct voters en route to the polls. The voter-hauling system did not work for Republicans. When an observer "asked the Democratic poll watcher to give a ride to St. Francis to a young Republican, Patrick Red Bird Wolfe, the Democratic poll worker responded that 'this is a partisan van pool, only for Democrats,' and refused to provide a ride to the young man."

After Hours

In one of the oddest twists in the election, the polls were kept open for an extra hour in Todd County, on the Rosebud Indian Reservation. Senator Johnson won Todd with 81 percent of the vote.

Early on Election Day, the Secretary of State's Office received demands from out-of-state Democratic lawyers claiming that because some stations had opened later than 7:00 A.M., the time set for the start of voting, they had to stay open later at night. This surprised Todd County auditor Kathleen Flakus, who twice in late October had published a notice in the local paper announcing that on Election Day the polls would be open from 7:00 A.M. until 7:00 P.M. Central Standard Time. It has been a tradition in Todd County to operate on Central Time, even though it is technically just west of the time-zone line that runs through South Dakota separating Central Time from Mountain Time (one hour earlier). Locals never give a thought to the discrepancy, but it caught the eye of some clever Democratic lawyers, who pounced on the ambiguity.

On Election Day, Iver Crow Eagle, a Democratic election official who was supposed to bring the ballot boxes to the St. Francis polling place in Todd County, showed up late, about 7:45 A.M. That meant the polling place didn't open until shortly before 8:00. This didn't bother the locals because the precinct could still stay open for a full twelve hours under a South Dakota law that allows the county auditor to keep any precinct open late if there has been an unforeseen delay.

But Democratic lawyers stationed in Todd County leaped on the incident to demand that *all* precincts in the heavily Democratic county be kept open an additional hour, and made a similar demand for next-door Mellette County, which also is west of the time line but keeps Central Time. The lawyers argued that the law required that the polls stay open until 7:00 P.M. Mountain Time, which meant staying open for a total of thirteen hours rather than twelve.

Local election officials couldn't believe the interference was occurring. "I said, 'Why should people have to vote on Mountain Time when they live by Central Time?'" says Kathleen Flakus, a Democrat. "To me, it just didn't make sense. And it still doesn't." But the out-of-state Democrats who had invaded the area were adamant. They argued with state officials, who were forced to concede that Todd and Mellette counties were, officially if not in any other way, in Mountain Time. "I got a call from the attorney general's office that said you will be open until 7:00 P.M. Mountain Time, and if we don't we'll be in violation of Section Five of the Voting Rights Act," Flakus later told the *National Review.*

Nancy Wanless, the Democratic election supervisor in Mission, recalls the Democratic poll watcher from California who was on site to insist that the polls stay open, and who "stuck her nose where it doesn't belong and I don't know what strings she pulled.... She makes phone calls and tells me that I am supposed to stay open until 8:00 P.M. [Central Time]. I said, 'I can't.' I was going by my book. She got mad and said, 'Well, you have to!'"

Local Republican leaders were paralyzed with indecision about what to do, recalls David Norcross, a lawyer from the Republican National Committee who had been sent to monitor the election. Late in the day, he finally convinced them to file suit to force the polls to close at the normal time. Their suit noted that state law requires that polling places be open from 7:00 A.M. to 7:00 P.M., meaning that the legislature clearly intended for voting booths to be open for twelve hours. "Allowing the polls to remain open thirteen rather than twelve hours would unconstitutionally and improperly dilute the votes of voters who voted during proper hours," the suit read. As a fallback position, the GOP requested that if the polls remained open, ballots cast after 7:00 P.M. Central Time be segregated from other ballots in case a judge later ruled in favor of the original closing time.

A state circuit-court judge dismissed the suit without comment, and the polls stayed open until 8:00 P.M. Central Time. Since the ballots were not segregated, it's not clear how many people voted during that critical extra hour, but it appears that the effect of the decision to keep the polls open in Todd and Mellette counties could have been significant in a close race. A witness in the Mission precinct stated that in the additional hour the polls were open, "50 additional votes were cast." At the St. Francis precinct, another witness reported that 22 additional votes were cast in the extra hour. If the average of 50 and 22 votes is multiplied by the number of precincts kept open for an extra hour (36 votes times 13 precincts), a total of 468 votes could have been cast during the extra hour of voting in Todd County. Less-populous Mellette County, which also had its polls open an extra hour, saw an unknown number of additional votes cast.

Hide-and-Seek Voters

Another problem on Election Day had to do with "hide-and-seek" voters. Poll workers reported witnessing at least thirty incidents where voters were allowed to vote after a suspicious exchange with election officials. Barry Jensen, a GOP poll watcher in Mellette County, reported:

On many occasions during the voting process, I observed voters who presented themselves to election judges by stating their names. The election judges advised these voters that the name given was not on the official list of registered voters. On many occasions the election judges would then read several names to these voters, asking questions such as, "could it be under" a name entirely different than the name given by the voter. On numerous occasions, these voters would eventually (after one or more alternate names were suggested by the election judge) agree that one of the names suggested was in fact such voter's name. All of these voters were permitted to vote.

The honor system that South Dakota had traditionally relied on had a gap in it big enough to drive a truckload of chads through. All that was required to register and vote in South Dakota in 2002 was a signature, a mailing address and a physical address. No identification was required. That made it difficult, if not impossible, for county auditors to determine that voters were properly registered and that they voted only once. As Attorney General Barnett said in July, "It's pretty easy to register under a false name, send in an absentee ballot request, vote and send in the ballot and get it counted." That's why in 2003, South Dakota adopted a law requiring an ID to vote. That law is now a source of bitter partisan warfare.

Improper Counting of Ballots

Some South Dakota counties may also have counted ballots incorrectly. As many as three hundred ballots from Shannon County, for example, may have been incorrectly counted. The blank spaces opposite a candidate's name on many Shannon ballots were not filled in and therefore the ballots were not properly marked, according to Lance Russell, the Fall River County state's attorney. South Dakota election law stipulates that "if the voting mark does not touch the circle or square and is not on or in the circle or square, the vote may not be counted." In Shannon, John Thune received 8 percent of the vote, a near-record low for a Republican, despite winning 50 percent of the vote statewide.

In Davison County, election officials improperly counted overvotes. On ballots where two Senate candidates had been marked, the election officials decided to block out the mark given to the candidate with the "lighter" mark. These marks were covered with small, round, white stickers. Election officials were videotaped blocking votes for Congressman Thune. Concerns were also raised in Davison County because operatives working for Senator Tim Johnson's office were initially granted access to the Democratic auditor's office and its computers without allowing similar access to other parties.

Interference with the Election Process

In addition to illegally distributing campaign literature and organizing voter-hauling efforts in the polling places, the numerous lawyers deployed by the Democrats were abusive throughout Election Day. "Some election board members claim the out-of-state poll watchers clearly interfered with their process," reported the *Todd County Tribune*. One poll watcher noted that a Democratic lawyer "told election officials that electioneering or reading materials could be brought into the polling place." When one election official made a call to the county auditor to find out if this was true, an out-of-state poll watcher belligerently demanded to know everything that had been said. Another challenged her as to whether she had even made the call.

Marilyn Fokkers of Mission has served on her local election board for decades, but she said it would be a long time before she would be willing to serve again. "Don't get me started!" she exclaimed, recalling Election Day 2002. Todd County auditor Kathleen Flakus agreed: "I've never spent such a miserable day in my life. I don't think I've recovered yet. All these attorneys!" At the St. Thomas precinct in Todd County, at least six Democratic poll watchers were scrutinizing voters who came to vote at St. Thomas Hall in Mission and challenging election board practices throughout the day. Some people pressured some of the local officials to accept questionable ballots and questionable voter identifications. An elderly poll watcher in Charles Mix County encountered a lawyer from Minneapolis, two law students and a law professor who challenged the absentee ballots being cast by members of the Greenwood and Clearfield Hutterite colonies, who vote heavily

Republican. In Shannon County, one observer was so abusive that police arrested him. The exhausted county auditor in Shannon County, after receiving a call from a polling place about yet another irregularity, simply said, "Just let the person vote so nobody gets shot down there."

Inducements to Vote

For years, Democrats had given out free tickets to Election Day picnics for voters on the Pine Ridge Sioux Reservation. George Cunningham, a former chief of staff to George McGovern, recalled that the McGovern campaign once gave reservation residents who had voted raffle tickets to win a free television. "But we weren't the only ones involved in something like that. There were a lot of places giving free food, and nothing was said," he told the *Sioux Falls Argus-Leader.* Other giveaways included free cigarettes.

These practices prompted U.S. attorney Karen Schreier, a Democrat, and Attorney General Mark Barnett, a Republican, to write an unusual joint letter to county auditors in 1998 noting that "simply offering to provide" food or gifts "in exchange for showing up to vote, is clearly against the law."

In 2002, this opinion was ignored. There is evidence that inducements to voters may have involved something more than merchandise. One witness said he saw cash exchanging hands between a Democratic poll watcher and the driver of a van used to transport Johnson's supporters to the polls. "Right in front of me at one point," he said. "I had another gentleman there with me and he called it to their attention, that it was inappropriate. I said to [a Democratic poll watcher], 'Boy you're spending a lot of money today' in reference to the vans—there must've been 50 vans on the reservation. He said money was not an object, that they had unlimited funds."

A Parmalee poll watcher, a retired highway patrol lieutenant, stated: "You know what the going rate was around here? Ten bucks." Three individuals in Todd County originally signed affidavits saying they were "given a ride to the polls in a van with Tim Johnson for Senate signs in the window ... [and] promised $10 if [they] would go vote," and, after receiving a ride back from the polling place, were "offered $10 for voting."

Two of the three individuals later changed their stories. The man linked to all three affidavits, Ed Charging Elk, claimed that the affidavits had become part of a "misunderstanding." But Charging Elk admitted that there "was discussion on the street about the $10," according to a report by the *Sioux Falls Argus-Leader.* "'I mentioned it to a couple of friends of mine. People on the streets were saying you go vote, they would give you gas money, $10, maybe a pack of cigarettes, and if you couldn't get there, they would give you a ride,' he said. That seemed to make sense to some of them, he said. 'That is normal procedure with tribal elections.'" Charging Elk also said that "Rosebud residents were a bit alarmed when a large group of outsiders converged on the reservation to begin a voter registration process. People were a little scared, nervous." Charging Elk did not know the visitors.

Charging Elk originally helped out when he was asked to register new voters. "I knew the people running Senator Johnson's office. They were paying people $1 apiece to register 1,000 names. I'm fairly well known around here, so I sat there one day for two hours with them about six weeks before the election, and I helped them with the addresses, where to find them, but I didn't charge them anything." At one point, however, he got fed up with the politicization of the reservations by Democrats. "I'm a Democrat, but I voted for John Thune."

The Race Card

Meanwhile, Democratic officials at the state level refused to provide reporters (including me) with information on the number of registrations and absentee ballot requests mailed from their offices. They also declined to document the number of people paid voter bounties. They responded to these questions by making claims of racism and voter suppression. Democratic spokeswoman Sarah Feinberg said, "It is clear that John Thune has engaged in a clear and concerted effort to discredit this registration drive and to suppress turnout on the reservations." Senator Daschle made similar charges: "We are now seeing a concerted Republican effort to make allegations and launch initiatives intended to suppress Native American voting."

Senator Tim Johnson equated the voter fraud search with Senator Trent Lott's statement that the nation would have been a better place if Senator Strom Thurmond had been elected president when he ran in 1948 on a segregationist platform. Referring to the statement, which caused Lott to lose his position as majority leader, Johnson said, "Senator Lott's remarks only served to divide Americans, just as some of the actions by Republican attorneys from Washington divided people in South Dakota with claims of voter fraud by Native Americans, claims that have been ruled to be fraudulent."

The racial scare tactics appear to have worked. Eight days after the election, John Thune announced he would not seek a recount or take other legal action to challenge the election. "Are there questions that need to be answered about the outcome of this election? I believe there are," he told supporters. "Did things happen that shouldn't have in some polling places around the state? I believe they did. Some of these issues would be resolved through a recount. However, others, though unethical, would not be righted through a recount."

Rather than contest the election and endure months of negative coverage painting him as a sore loser, Thune decided instead to challenge Senator Daschle himself in the 2004 election and has spent a great deal of time building relationships on Indian reservations he barely visited in 2002.

"Democrats charged Republicans with racism and a conspiracy to prevent Native American voting," says Ron Williamson, president of the Great Plains Public Policy Institute. "It worked in that no one wanted to go through the ugliness that would have ensued from an election challenge." But it also may have convinced Republicans that they need to make an appeal to voters they aren't automatically comfortable in courting.

Conclusion

South Dakota isn't Chicago or South Texas. Prior to 2002, the state's elections were largely clean. But with the political polarization of America intensifying and control of the U.S. Senate hanging in the balance, a flood of outside money and workers from both parties entered the state. Like other states its size, South Dakota didn't have sufficient safeguards in place to ensure the integrity of the election. Most polling places were run by little old ladies and good-government volunteers. They weren't ready for the aggressive onslaught that confronted them on Election Day.

The 2002 election was a lacerating experience and it is no exaggeration to say that South Dakota will never be the same. The GOP-controlled state legislature voted in 2003 to require all voters to show an ID, a measure that Secretary of State Chris Nelson estimates 75 percent of the population supports. But Democrats have savaged the law as racist and vowed to file suit to have it annulled.

Meanwhile, in the run-up to the 2004 elections, problems have again surfaced. Two felons were revealed to be receiving payments to register only Democrats in Rapid City in April 2004. Kea Warne, the elections supervisor for the secretary of state's office, said, "We were informed they'd get more for a Democrat, less for an independent and nothing for a Republican." Another man in Rapid City who was being paid to register Democrats was found to have previously been convicted of murder in the state of Washington. The same month, a man was charged and found guilty of voter registration fraud in Watertown, South Dakota, and a prison inmate was found to have registered to vote in Sioux Falls. Auditors' offices were also receiving registrations in large envelopes with no return address, which generated additional suspicions.

After a June 1 special election for the U.S. House, a nonprofit Indian voting rights group, Four Directions, filed federal civil-rights lawsuits when reports surfaced that about forty people on Indian reservations claimed they were denied a ballot because they lacked a photo ID. They said they had not been offered the opportunity to sign an affidavit, a backup measure provided for in the voter ID law passed in 2003. In response, Senator Daschle promptly started the "Daschle Voting Rights Project" to prevent efforts to exclude Indians from the polls. Daschle also sent a widely publicized letter to the secretary of state about people "being denied the right to vote" and "harassment" on the reservations. Secretary Nelson says he still supports the photo ID law because it both protects against fraudulent votes and ensures that all qualified voters will be allowed to cast ballots. Voters can show a variety of forms of photo identification, and if they lack that, they can sign the affidavits. "If there were problems the first time ever the law was implemented in the primary, we will fix that with better training," he says.

Everyone supports making certain that people's right to vote is fully protected, and that any vestiges of the days of poll taxes or literacy tests are stamped out. But dubious charges of racism or intimidation at the polls make it difficult to police the integrity of elections. People who don't want their good names sullied try to stay out of the line of fire, even if they have legitimate questions about the fairness of the election process. There is also the chance that members of the party accused of racism will respond to what they perceive as election irregularities not being properly policed by authorities with their own examples of corner-cutting. A vicious cycle of charges, countercharges and recriminations can soon transform even the most placid of states into a bitter battleground in a short time, as South Dakota has seen.

CHAPTER SEVEN

Tropical Tammany

As those of us who have been there know, Hawaii is a warm and welcoming paradise saturated by a radiant sun and surrounded by sapphire seas. Cool trade winds sweep the island chain and a friendly "Aloha" spirit among its people makes it heaven for vacationers. What visitors don't see, however, is that the Aloha spirit doesn't penetrate the closed doors and smoke-filled rooms of local and state politics. Hawaii has the worst public education system and nearly the highest high school dropout rates in the nation. Its tax burden is the fourth-highest, its per capita debt the second. It has the highest property crime rate of all fifty states. More pertinent for the issue at hand, it has the worst voter turnout rate. It also has a persistent problem with voting irregularities, the legacy of being dominated by a one-party machine that calls to mind New York's infamous Tammany Hall from the bad old days. The Democratic machine controlled all the levers of state government for forty straight years until the 2002 election of a Republican governor began to expose cracks in its façade.

The new administration has its work cut out for it. The British magazine *The Economist* concluded that Hawaii "is a lousy place to do business. Not only is the cost of living roughly a third higher than the American urban average, but government is far more centralized than in other states." In 2002, *Forbes* magazine gave Hawaii the "Booby Prize for Economic Development" and the title of its article summed up the feelings of most Hawaii business people: "Trouble in Paradise: Why doing business in Honolulu has become nearly equivalent to suicide." Businesses have to contend with some of the strictest regulations and most burdensome mandates in the country. A unique, regressive and pyramiding tax—the General Excise Tax—takes around 4 percent on goods at every level of production, and is the equivalent of a sales tax of about 12 to 16 percent. Each year, the state legislature, dominated by Democrats for the past four decades, achieves the seemingly impossible distinction of worsening the already disastrous business climate.

Former governor Benjamin J. Cayetano is blamed for creating much of the damage during his eight years in office, from 1995 to 2003. Deemed an "American Caesar" by political columnist George Will, Cayetano boasted in public speeches that his philosophy was to "punish your enemies and reward your friends," and he did just that, showering his closest friends with generous non-bid contracts and aggressively using the power of the government to put enemies out of business. Loyal friends like Earl Anzai received well-paid state administrative appointments. After being ousted as budget director by the state senate, Anzai was appointed by Governor Cayetano as the attorney general, the state's highest law enforcement officer.

Despite warnings from the state's most powerful politician, U.S. Senator Daniel Inouye, who told his own Democratic Party at its 1998 state convention that it was growing increasingly vindictive, bloated and arrogant, Governor Cayetano continued to target people he perceived as enemies, including journalists, educators and "dissident" Democrats. He was able to rule with an iron hand because the structure of Hawaii's centralized government keeps most functions and financial revenue streams under state government control instead of directed to county or city jurisdictions as in other states. Cayetano was also able to fill by appointment positions that typically are elected in other states, such as state judges, the state attorney general, his administrators and deputies, and appointees to various commissions and boards. His adversaries saw firsthand his swift and strong retaliation against people he specifically targeted.

"He is a governor who attacked every messenger of bad economic news," says state senator Sam Slom, a Republican from east Oahu Island. Senator Slom, who also heads the group Small Business Hawaii, says that Governor Cayetano held publications such as the *Wall Street Journal, Forbes* and *The Economist* in contempt, calling them all "ultra right wing publications that no one listens to anyway." Cayetano even accused the world's leading bond rating service, Moody's, of being politically motivated and biased after it issued its assessment of Hawaii's finances. Lowell Kalapa, president of the Tax Foundation of Hawaii, says the biggest disappointment with Cayetano's time in office was that at a period in history when the people of the state most needed to be united, they did not have someone to bring them together. Instead, Cayetano polarized the community.

The 1998 Election Fiasco

In 1998, the faltering economy and the incompetence of state government combined to create a climate in which Republican Linda Lingle, former mayor of Maui, stood to defeat Governor Cayetano as he ran for reelection. The final polls in the state's major papers had Mayor Lingle favored by a considerable margin. That is one reason why there was a cloud of suspicion over the general election when Cayetano won by a slim margin of only 5,000 votes, or about 1.5 percent of the vote. Many people reported instances of fraud or irregularities to the state Office of Elections, the U.S. Attorney's Office and the Federal Bureau of Investigation, hoping they would launch an independent probe. Complaints were made of vote buying by at least one Democratic politician. There were also large spikes in absentee voting in some districts, reports of noncitizens and dead people voting, electioneering by poll watchers and the general public in the polling places, and boxes of ballots disappearing, then arriving in unsealed containers at the counting center.

While the majority of media largely ignored the complaints of voting irregularities and fraud, reporters could not ignore what came next. On the heels of the suspiciously narrow victory, Cayetano and Democratic Party members were not pleased when the local representative for Election Systems & Software (ES&S), the Texas-based company providing the voting machines for Hawaii's 1998 election, announced that they had discovered problems. ES&S admitted that during the general election, machines in at least seven precincts had malfunctioned. Though ES&S had recently experienced serious technical problems in Venezuela, Canada and four American states, the company broadcast blame for the malfunctions, launching accusations at Hawaii's "ignorant poll workers," "ignorant voters" and even "piggish voters" who apparently brought food into the voting booths and it fell into the machines. In addition, ES&S announced that its machines had a 1 percent margin of error, meaning they could not guarantee that the election results were accurate within plus or minus 1 percent.

Because there is no automatic recount provision in Hawaii law (it has been consistently voted down by the state legislature, including a vote in 2004), it looked as though Hawaii voters were just going to have to settle with the results they got. Then, without informing the media, the candidates or the public, the state's chief elections officer, Dwayne Yoshina, began in secret to organize a manual recount of ballots from some of the seven precincts. One of these was Waianae, a beautiful but poor community on the west side of Oahu, whose people had elected Democrat Colleen Hanabusa, an aggressive attorney and outspoken advocate for her community, as their state senator. Hanabusa shook Hawaii's political world before her election results were even certified when she learned that Yoshina was recounting the ballots from her race, but was not planning to allow her to be present for the recount. At her urging, the state senate convened a special investigation to determine whether more than just the seven known precincts with balloting problems had been affected by glitches in the ES&S software. That investigation led to the first-ever recount of nearly all of Hawaii's general election ballots.

In Waianae precinct 44–01, for example, there were 157 overvotes (more than one candidate marked for an office) in the state house of representatives race, 122 in the state senate race, 107 in the gubernatorial contest, 118 for U.S. House of Representatives, and 38 for U.S. Senate. But even if manual recounts showed that the losing candidate actually won in the districts in question, it was unlikely that the final tally would be overturned because of the state's extremely short, twenty-day appeals period, which had ended on November 23, 1998.

Under Hawaii law, it is up to the candidate or other plaintiff to show proof of errors that would change the results of the election. Otherwise, they must demonstrate that the correct results cannot be ascertained because of a mistake or fraud on the part of the precinct officials. Senator Hanabusa maintained that she wasn't interested in overturning announced results, just clearing the dark cloud from the 1998 election. She wanted to make sure that future elections were operated in a sound manner.

ES&S did not like the mounting public criticism, which reached hurricane force during the state senate hearings. The company's top executives threatened to sue two Republican representatives who testified before the Hawaii Senate Judiciary Committee with complaints about the ES&S software glitches, apparently not realizing that under state law, those testifying are protected from lawsuits. Tom Eschberger, the vice president of ES&S, also wrote scathing rebuttals to journalists over their stories on the voting machine failures and threatened national media outlets with lawsuits for their articles. "The fact is that, no matter how good your hardware, software and support, if you remain in the industry long enough, you will have elections that do not go the way you or the customer would like, particularly when there is a radical change in systems," Eschberger said. He countered criticism by saying that 60 percent of the votes cast in the United States in the 1998 elections were cast on ES&S systems, and that problems with software in cities such as Detroit, Dallas and Providence, Rhode Island, were eventually cleared up.

But even with adamant denials and threats of lawsuits against critics, ES&S had difficulty fending off the numerous investigations. The involvement of Mr. Eschberger in a bribery scandal, though he was not convicted or arrested, was widely reported in the media. One national voter-related Web site noted in an editorial: "It just doesn't look good for a voting machine company to have a vice president take an immunity plea in a case related to election matters." The states of California and Florida investigated the company for conflict-of-interest issues.

Despite Hawaii's problems and the serious failures of the ES&S software in other locations both in the United States and abroad, Hawaii's chief elections officer remained surprisingly loyal to ES&S. Hawaiians weren't prepared for the newspaper headlines that ran shortly after the recount of nearly all the ballots from the 1998 general election: ES&S was once again awarded, without open bidding, an exclusive contract to run Hawaii's elections for the next eight years. Competitors to ES&S, including two companies that dropped out of the bidding process, said they could not have competed for the contract because the specifications provided by the Office of Elections were written so that only ES&S could qualify.

Senator Hanabusa said the decision-making process and the lack of competitive bidding in the selection of the election vendor showed the need for oversight of the chief elections officer: "I just can't believe that this is what happened and this is how the decision was made." Yet Yoshina insisted in statements to the media that the state got a good deal. Eschberger said that ES&S had lost a great deal of money on the Hawaii contract and the company was pleased that a long-term contract would help it recoup its loss.

Voting Integrity Project

Other problems plagued the 1998 election, yet Hawaii's law enforcement, including the attorney general appointed by Governor Cayetano, were not interested in pursuing allegations of fraud.

Hawaii has a history of election fraud going back at least to 1982, when the political and legal community was shocked by a voter registration scandal involving University of Hawaii law school students who illegally registered voters for a Democratic candidate for the state house, Ross Segawa. They were caught when volunteers for his opponent noticed that these youthful supporters of Segawa were registered at the Arcadia Retirement Residence. An investigation by the city prosecutor's office led to Segawa's conviction on ten counts of election fraud, criminal solicitation and evidence tampering, for which he served sixty days in prison.

Clifford Uwaine, a former state senator also involved in the Segawa scandal, was convicted of conspiring to register voters illegally and served three months in jail. Debra Kawaoka, an aide to

Uwaine who also played a part in the false registration scandal, served numerous weekends in jail. In another case of election fraud, an Oahu grand jury indicted state legislator Gene Albano in 1983 for illegally registering voters in his Kalihi Kai-Iwilei House District, and a decade later he was finally convicted of voter registration fraud. (Albano served two terms in the state house before his defeat in his 1984 reelection bid.)

Governor Cayetano pardoned both Segawa and Albano in 2000 and appointed several other students in the University of Hawaii law school voter registration scandal to high-ranking government jobs. Brian Minaii, for example, was appointed director of the Department of Transportation. Other law students went on to work in law enforcement in the attorney general's and city prosecutor's offices. Patrick Pascual, who provided the initial statements to the Honolulu prosecutor in 1982 in exchange for immunity, is a deputy attorney general, as is Edsel Yamada, who was chairman of Segawa's 1982 campaign.

But what happened in 1998 was extreme even by Hawaii's standards. Allegations of voting irregularities and fraud prompted the nonprofit Voting Integrity Project to open an investigation. Based in Washington, D.C., the group was formed to protect election integrity by providing recount monitors, registration cleanup programs and poll watching free of charge to communities. It had investigated and helped to prosecute numerous election officials, state officials and campaign volunteers for fraud.

Founder Deborah Phillips said then that VIP was interested in several election irregularities discovered while four of its investigators were in Hawaii in March 1999 for the recount of the ballots cast in the 1998 election. VIP hired two retired FBI agents based in Hawaii, Cal Uhlig and Hilton Loui, to investigate the horror stories that the organization had heard. Working in conjunction with an informal underground group of former law enforcement and computer experts, the agents decided to focus on three areas: aliens voting, absentee ballot fraud and fraudulent voting in elderly care homes. Other irregularities, such as unions influencing their members through absentee voting at work and reported dead voters, were put aside. Loui and Uhlig homed in on Districts 29 to 31 on Oahu, among others, which had dramatic spikes in absentee voting. (Hawaii reported that an abnormally high 18 percent of its ballots were cast absentee in the 1998 general election, with many districts exceeding 35 percent absentee voting.)

In Districts 29, 30 and 31, impoverished areas of Oahu where many noncitizens reside, there was an unusual voting pattern. In one of the districts, around a thousand people voted by absentee ballot on the same day, and returned their ballots by mail in unison two weeks later. Many of these people lived in a six-block area, with some homes housing up to ten residents with five different family names. Upon closer examination of the actual ballots, VIP investigators found that a number of them were filled out in the same handwriting. Some of the signatures were completely illegible, but what stood out to investigators was that the signature line on many ballots bore just a simple "X." (When questioned about the "X" signatures on absentee ballots, election officials said that for those who cannot sign their name, an "X" is a valid signature.)

VIP investigators learned through canvassing that Representative Romy Cachola, a Democrat who in 2000 won a Honolulu City Council seat, is notorious in his Kalihi District for efforts to "get out the vote" through absentee mail ballots. In 1998, Cachola's district saw nearly 40 percent of voters cast absentee ballots, one of the highest rates in any district. That rate climbed even higher in 2000. Statistics from the state Office of Elections show that Cachola wouldn't have won some of his extremely close elections without these key votes.

Cachola adamantly denied any wrongdoing in a letter to HawaiiReporter.com, the Web site that broke the story about irregularities in his district and elsewhere. However, the state Campaign Spending Commission saw another issue raised by HawaiiReporter.com in the Cachola election that was worth investigating. Cachola listed dozens of "PR expenses" or "donations" under his expenditure reports, in many cases without addresses or first names of the recipients. All of the public relations expenses and donations were $20, $30, $45, $50 or $100. Though numerous, these expenditures were rather insignificant compared with his overall campaign fund—between $150,000 and $250,000, one of the highest campaign funds in the Honolulu City Council; but the Campaign Spending Commission wanted an explanation of monies that his spending report admitted were given out before the primary and general elections to people such as:

- Edward Fontanilla. No address listed. Donation $50
- Juanito Castro. No address listed. Donation $50
- Moses Imperial. No listed address. Donation $30
- C. Miguel. No address listed. Donation $50
- Quirino III Galicia. Donation $30

VIP investigators also uncovered a number of confirmed noncitizens and suspected noncitizens who voted in Cachola's district. That led them to encourage the Honolulu city clerk, Genny Wong, to figure out a way to determine if more noncitizens were voting throughout the state. The federal Immigration and Naturalization Service, run by the Clinton administration, refused to help in the assessment. But that did not deter Wong and her staff, who independently cross-referenced names on the state's registered voter rolls with the citizenship records in the state's identification database, and determined that 543 registered voters on Oahu may have been or still are improperly or illegally registered to vote.

Wong sent out letters to those suspected 543 alien registered voters asking for proof of citizenship. More than a hundred people responded shortly after Wong's inquiry, with about half providing proof and the other half asking that their names be removed from the voter registration rolls.

This was the city's first extensive effort to find out who may be illegally registered in Hawaii, and it is important to note that the city checked only those who had state identifications (not driver's licenses), a small part of the population in Hawaii. City officials said that a small number of neighbor islanders who held state identifications also were listed as noncitizens and would be issued letters.

No Political Will to Prosecute

The Honolulu City Council chairman at the time, Jon Yoshimura, who called a press conference in 1999 to announce the findings, said it is possible that the noncitizens registered to vote had in fact

voted in recent elections, but were not likely to face any consequences for doing so. He said he believes that further investigation is needed as to who is improperly registered and why, but it
is not the city council's role to take on such an investigation. He
also emphasized in interviews with the press that the city should
"tread lightly" and not go on a "witch hunt."

The city's announcement spurred a flurry of criticism in the
local media by some noncitizens and their supporters who claimed
they should be able to vote in Hawaii elections, whether or not
they are citizens. State representative Dennis Arakaki, a Democrat,
slammed the city for its "heavy-handed" tactics, for sending a "very
intimidating and threatening kind of letter" and for presuming
that the state ID database is accurate. He also maintained that
Hawaii's noncitizens are often more interested in and excited about
the democratic process than Hawaii's citizens.

Governor Cayetano—who had insisted all along that there
was no fraud in the 1998 election, even to the point of ridiculing
those who made such claims—said he would ask his attorney general to probe deeper into city findings. Not surprisingly, no men-
tion was ever made of that putative investigation by the attorney
general, and Cayetano continued to defend the chief elections officer, Dwayne Yoshina, in the face of criticism that he had not run a
vigorous investigation of abuses. For his part, Yoshina defended
the alien voters, saying they must have honestly thought they were
citizens. Misunderstandings and innocent mistakes are the likely
explanation in most cases, Yoshina averred, telling the press that
the whole issue was "complicated."

U.S. attorney Steve Alm did not ask his deputies to investigate the case further, notwithstanding public and media requests
to do so, and he was rewarded upon leaving his position in 2000
when Cayetano named him a state judge.

The Immigration and Naturalization Service also refused to
help the city or VIP investigators, although a story surfaced in the
Honolulu Advertiser later in 1999 about three noncitizens who had
voted in the 1998 election, were subsequently caught by the INS
and eventually were deported. The INS declined to provide any
further information.

The Governor Retaliates

In the fall of 1999, enough time had elapsed that Governor Cayetano felt safe to begin focusing on those individuals who had helped to prompt the investigation into the 1998 election as well as those who had openly supported Mayor Lingle's candidacy over his own. Several business owners who openly supported the Republican candidates in 1998 and the recount, as well as Democrats who spoke out against their party, said they were being harassed and intimidated by government officials. They strongly suspect their activism led to investigations by state agencies including the Hawaii Occupational Safety and Health division of the Department of Labor and Industrial Relations, the state attorney general, the state Department of Taxation, and the Department of Health's inspection division.

A series of articles in 1998 and 1999 by investigative reporter Malia Zimmerman in *Pacific Business News* documented the alleged retribution. Zimmerman interviewed Kitty Lagareta, a former Democrat who worked for Mayor Lingle in the 1998 gubernatorial election, who experienced her share of retaliation. Ms. Lagareta was subpoenaed twice by the state attorney general, was told by Hawaii Occupational Safety and Health division administrators that she was at the "top of the list" for its investigators, and was threatened with litigation by a company closely affiliated with the state Office of Elections. (Lagareta went on to serve on an elections review panel in an attempt to further reforms in Hawaii's election system.)

Linda Smith, then treasurer of the Hawaii Republican Party and co-owner with her husband Paul of the 35-year-old company Pacific Allied Products, was investigated shortly after the 1998 elections by the tax department, the state and federal occupational safety agencies, the Department of Health and the Honolulu Fire Department. All turned up no violations. (Smith soon afterward sold her business and in 2004 was named the senior policy adviser to Governor Linda Lingle.)

Ed Medeiros, owner of the Aloha Flea Market, the oldest and largest swap meet in the state, had promoted Mayor Lingle's gubernatorial candidacy along with his nine hundred vendors in 1998.

He subsequently lost his right to lease the state's Aloha Stadium. Governor Cayetano's cousin-in-law, local defense attorney Michael Green, headed up the stadium council that voted to boot Medeiros.

Through her own investigation, Malia Zimmerman also uncovered a number of irregularities in the 1998 elections, leading VIP to open an investigation in Hawaii. For her efforts, she too experienced Governor Cayetano's wrath. In November 1999, Cayetano and his communications director, Jackie Kido, filed a formal complaint on the governor's letterhead with the Honolulu Media Council (a council with essentially no legal power composed of fifty-one Democrats and one Republican). They charged that *Pacific Business News* "continuously ignored journalistic ethics by willfully engaging in the practice of manipulating information and knowingly reporting inaccurate, unbalanced and unsubstantiated stories. From printing unfounded accusations against State government alleging 'acts of retribution' to knowingly presenting false government documents ..." In a brazen effort to censure and silence PBN, Cayetano and Kido said they had acted "after having received a series of complaints from State government officials regarding the journalistic practices of PBN" and "on behalf of the public servants that have been maligned, and the citizenry that has unduly lost faith in their government." They further accused PBN of being "a partner in a scheme" to print a false government document (the small-business task force report documenting complaints against the Cayetano administration by around three hundred businesses). They claimed that PBN had failed to take any action to correct the problems and alleged that PBN's stories were "deceitful and wrong." Cayetano reportedly applied pressure against PBN's advertisers, and continued to pressure the paper to send Zimmerman to ethics training and to apologize publicly.

In April 2000, just months before the 2000 election,. Zimmerman won a national award from the Voting Integrity Project for her investigative reporting, which was presented to her in Washington, D.C. PBN suddenly changed its position, went through her computer and personal files, and accused her of "collaborating" with activists on voting fraud stories. Zimmerman was placed on forced "vacation."

On May 22, the *Wall Street Journal* published an editorial entitled "Hawaii's Gray Politics," which documented the retaliation against many critics of the governor, including Malia Zimmerman. PBN editor Gina Mangeri accused Ms. Zimmerman of ghosting the unsigned editorial, and, claiming that she was "too high maintenance," gave her a chance to resign. Zimmerman refused and was fired.

Kido sent out a letter on the governor's stationery to all Hawaii media announcing the firing. In an attempt to blackball her from the media marketplace, Kido announced that the governor would withdraw his complaint if Zimmerman was not rehired within the next twelve months. When applying for jobs in the local media, Zimmerman discovered that word from the governor's office preceded her visits. Many in Hawaii believe the governor's retaliation was an attempt to prevent her from further investigating election fraud in Hawaii as well as the vendetta by the governor's office against his critics.

Two years later, in 2002, Zimmerman and another former coworker from *Pacific Business News* launched HawaiiReporter.com, which today investigates corruption in government and business along with voting irregularities.

Defending the Status Quo

In 2002, Linda Lingle ran again for governor and defeated Lieutenant Governor Mazie Hirono by an unambiguous 16,000 votes. After being sworn in, she soon moved to oust Dwayne Yoshina as the chief elections officer. But Democrats had a different plan. They wanted to protect Yoshina, who was clearly aligned with the Democrat Party, and keep him in that position—and they could do so because they still had control of the Elections Appointment and Review Commission, consisting of three Democratic appointees and two Republicans.

In 2003, the three Democratic commission members refused to allow others to apply for Yoshina's position, saying they knew he was unquestionably the best person for the job. They also refused a request by the governor's office to advertise the position in the local and mainland papers. They sent an evaluation form to Yoshina supporters, and then claimed he got rave reviews—although the vast majority of the political community did not even know they could participate in the evaluation process.

Some members of the Elections Review Task Force, a separate nine-member panel appointed by the governor and lawmakers in 2001 to study problems with Hawaii's election system, admitted they were completely frustrated by Yoshina's conduct of his office. They blamed him for intentionally coming unprepared to the semimonthly meetings so that issues were not resolved. "It is pretty frustrating. He thinks we will burn out and quit if he wastes our time and the committee never gets anything done. And he is probably right—some of us will probably quit," Kitty Lagareta, then a member of the task force and CEO of Communications-Pacific, Inc., told HawaiiReporter.com, "Most of the time he just tells us why our suggestions won't work. He is now coming back to say our work on the committee is done, but it is not. There are many more important things to address." The panel was eventually dissolved without Yoshina or the legislature recommending any of its suggestions.

In September, Yoshina was reappointed to another four-year term as the state's chief elections officer by the Elections Appointment and Review Commission on a three-to-two vote, divided strictly along party lines. Kimo Sutton, a six-year commissioner appointed by the Republican minority in the state house of representatives, maintained that the vote was unexpected, not on the agenda, and illegal. He wasn't even notified that the issue of Yoshina's reappointment was going to be discussed until the night before, and he was never told the appointment would be voted on as part of "new business." The state's attorney general later determined that the reappointment, while not handled properly, would stand.

Ray Pua, chairman of the Elections Appointment and Review Commission, told his fellow commission members why it wasn't a good idea to replace Yoshina: "We would be accepting a student when we could rehire the teacher." To further insulate Yoshina from criticism and attempts to remove him, in May 2004 the Democratic legislature passed a law creating another elections commission to oversee him.

Elections for the state legislature will be held in November 2004, with Republicans struggling to increase their minority of 5 out of 25 state senators and 15 out of 51 representatives. Even though there is more of a balance of power in state government, there still is virtually no protection against voter fraud and no way for the public to hold the elections commissioner accountable or gain access to information to investigate irregularities.

Lawmakers say that election officials will have the full voter list and will be able to detect any fraud, such as voting outside of home districts. But critics say there is no guarantee that officials have the interest, time or political will to detect election misconduct and then pursue an investigation. Hawaii's history as an electoral bamboo republic indicates that they are probably right.

"We would never guard our currency at the U.S. Mint the way we guard the currency of democracy—votes."
—Computer systems engineer David Allen

CHAPTER EIGHT

High-Tech Voting

With the exception of the 2000 Florida fiasco, the biggest collection of conspiracy theories about our national elections centers around the direct-recording electronic machines (DREs) that thirty-five million Americans will be using to record their votes in November 2004.

These machines are designed to remedy the chads and dimples and butterfly ballots that made voting for president so chaotic in Florida during the 2000 election. In an effort to design a new system before the next president is elected, many states, including Florida and its neighbor Georgia, have installed DREs, which instantly record and tabulate votes. Some even use fancy touch-screen technology similar to automated teller machines in banks. But the machines have become the latest punching bag in the mutual war of suspicion over which side is trying to steal elections.

It is necessary to put the paranoia about computer voting into perspective by remembering that every election system is subject to fraud and errors. Paper ballots were so abused in the nineteenth century that lever voting machines were developed. Bosses in Chicago and other places soon learned how to add votes by turning the wheels at the back of the machine, leaving no evidence of their handiwork. The punch-card machines and optical scanners that replaced these lever machines in the 1960s in many places had problems with the subjective reading of improperly filled-out ballots; and as we've already seen in abundant detail, ballots could easily be altered or voided while they were transported to a central counting station.

As the latest technology, DREs bring with them a separate set of concerns. Some computer scientists are alarmed by the possibility that unscrupulous programmers could manipulate the new machines. Internal documents from Diebold Election Systems, which has sold more than 33,000 touch-screen DRE machines, acknowledge that there have been security flaws, although the company denies that these flaws could allow a hacker to cast multiple votes or alter the votes of others, as some critics of the new technology suggest. Diebold insists that the problems have been or are being fixed, but the company is haunted by the perception (in part created preemptively by Democratic operatives) that Walden O'Dell, the chairman and CEO of Diebold (and a major Bush contributor), is a Republican stooge planning to use his company's software to tilt the election count. O'Dell's activism and six-figure contributions by Diebold to Republicans have set off a frenzy of conspiracy chat on the Internet.

Bev Harris, a 52-year-old freelance journalist from Seattle, has led a crusade against the new technology ever since she learned that Georgia had become the first state to replace all its old machines with shiny new DREs from Diebold. She became convinced that the results of the Georgia Senate race lost by incumbent Democrat Max Cleland in 2002 were suspect. Her only evidence was that Cleland had led in the final pre-election poll by five points but wound up losing by seven. (Cleland himself says the campaign against him was dirty, but acknowledges that he lost fairly. He says it's a good thing Georgia led the nation in adopting statewide electronic voting.)

But through her sleuthing Harris did turn up some gold when, in surfing the Internet, she happened upon 40,000 unprotected computer files owned by Diebold. The Internet files included material on its Global Election Management System tabulation software, source codes for Diebold's AccuVote touch-screen voting machine, a Texas voter registration list, and live vote data from fifty-seven precincts in a 2002 California primary election.

Harris also learned from her perusal of the files that Diebold machines sold to the State of Georgia could be accessed with a "supervisor smart card" and that every one of the 22,000 machines had the same entry password: 1111. State officials had the machines tested by two independent labs, which approved them. But Harris questions how independent the labs are since one of them gave $25,000 to the Republican National Committee in 2000.

Out of these facts and factoids was born a conspiracy theory that is bound to grow in magnitude and influence because so much of our overall electoral system is indeed in a sorry state.

A Democrat Punctures the Conspiracy Balloon

Joe Andrew was chairman of the Democratic National Committee until Bill Clinton left office in 2001. He is also the only chairman of a national political party who has ever come from a technology background, having been a partner in a biotechnology firm that owned several Internet companies. He considers himself a Democrat with a foot in both the party establishment and the growing progressive movement that congregated around Howard Dean. "I own both an Oldsmobile and a Blackberry," he jokes.

But Andrew says the conspiracy theories surrounding electronic voting are no laughing matter. In June 2004 he gave a speech to the Maryland Association of Election Officials that ripped the bark off the "black box" conspiracy theorists. "When it comes to electronic voting, most liberals are just plain old-fashioned nuts," he told the election officials. While conservatives were skilled at coordinating their messages and agendas, "that does not mean there is a vast right-wing conspiracy trying to steal votes in America, as the loudest voices on the left are saying today."

Andrew divided the people who were obsessed about a DRE stolen election into two groups: computer experts with impressive technical experience but little practical experience with elections, and progressive computer users who are conspiratorial by nature. He claims they have been joined in their hysteria by the Democratic Party and prominent members of Congress who "are rallying behind the anti-DRE bandwagon in a big election year because they think that this movement is good for Democrats."

Sadly, he says the people they are hurting are mostly Democrats. "Any Democrat who thinks that getting rid of direct electronic voting machines will help the Democrats win is simply out to lunch," he told the election officials. He noted that the Leadership Conference on Civil Rights has generally supported electronic voting because study after study has found that the voters who are most likely to be helped by DREs are: a) the disabled (they can vote without assistance); b) the less-educated (the machines resemble the ubiquitous ATM); c) lower socioeconomic groups (who often trust machines more than people); d) the truly elderly (you can increase the type size) and citizens more comfortable voting in a language other than English.

Indeed, as many problems as DREs have, they must be assessed in comparison with the other existing systems. In California's 2003 recall election, the largest election conducted since the 2002 midterms, punch-card systems failed to record a valid vote on 6.3 percent of all ballots cast. For optical scan systems, the rate was 2.7 percent, and for DREs the rate was only 1.5 percent. If accuracy was our only goal, then DREs were almost twice as accurate as the next available technology.

As for the theories about how DREs could be programmed to change an election, Andrew maintained that "it is not possible to move a constant fraction of votes from one party to another in each jurisdiction without it being obvious that something is going on." He concluded that "the liberal Internet activists are bonkers."

Or maybe not. By whipping up a frenzy of suspicion about electronic voting, Democrats will have built a platform from which, if the presidential or key Senate elections in November 2004 are close, they can launch endless lawsuits everywhere there were problems with electronic machines. Senator John Kerry has already announced the formation of a legal SWAT team of election lawyers that will be deployed all over the country to challenge election results. This "election through litigation" strategy could stretch the dispute over the 2004 election for weeks or months and increase the cynicism of Americans about the validity of our elections even more. If you hated Florida in 2000, you may not have seen anything yet.

Inside the Black Box

Direct-recording electronic machines are polarizing gadgets. One side sees a security and reliability nightmare, and predicts they will deliver chaos in the November 2004 election, including suspicions that these "black boxes" will either add or eat votes depending on which candidate some "Manchurian Programmer" wants to win. The other side sees DREs as the most modern machines available, offering a significantly lower rate of ballot spoilage than other technologies, including paper.

As for security, the source code used to program any machine can be open for inspection to enough people that any anomaly will be caught. Most importantly, the machines are *not* hooked up to the Internet; they are stand-alone machines. "Hackers can do anything only in books and movies," says Michael Shamos, a professor of computer science at Carnegie Mellon University who served as Pennsylvania's examiner of electronic voting systems for twenty years. "The prospect that a hacker could not only manipulate an election but do it without employing a detectable bug is so far-fetched an idea no one has come close to showing how it might be done."

There certainly are problems with DREs that demand attention. Some of the voting machine companies that produce them have dubious records of competence or integrity, and demand more scrutiny by both the media and election officials. Some states have rushed to buy new equipment that they don't know how to operate, and they didn't insist on getting a copy of the computer software used in the machines. Many devices will inevitably break down in the November 2004 election and cause long lines, unhappy voters and even more conspiracy theories.

But breakdowns don't equal conspiracy. Susan Zevin, the former deputy director of the Commerce Department's National Institute of Standards and Technology, says there is "absolutely no evidence" that an election has been altered by fraud in an electronic system. The nightmare scenarios conjured up by Harris and her Internet allies can be completely prevented if the machines are rigorously tested by outsiders. Zevin says the computer experts who side with Harris are very knowledgeable but have almost zero experience in election administration. "It's easy in a laboratory to write a program that throws an election," she notes, "but you don't have elections in a laboratory."

Most electronic voting machines transfer the election results to a compact disk or some other "read only" format. These CDs are then taken to a central location where they are read into a computer. Breaking into each machine one at a time without breaking the tamper-proof seals and being detected is possible but highly unlikely. In the twenty-plus years that these machines have been used, in many counties all across the country, there has never been a verified case of tampering.

What about the nightmare scenario that Diebold's Walden O'Dell will secretly program the computers to alter the election results? Audit devices and parallel testing regimes should accompany any machine to make sure any such manipulation is caught. Professor Shamos says "the manipulations of any vendor can be made fruitless if we separate the candidate and party names from the capture and recording logic of the computer program. A vendor or hacker won't know who he is helping or hurting."

It's true that in Maryland, computer experts hired by election officials to test the security of the state's individual Diebold machines easily hacked into the DREs, either directly or through telephone lines. The machines failed the test completely. Yet the tampering wasn't under real-world conditions. An old system was used, and although the hackers succeeded in their break-in, the original data in the voting machines were not compromised; in the real world it would still have been possible to conduct an accurate recount.

Britain J. Williams, a retired professor of computer science who has spent eighteen years evaluating computer-based voting systems for the State of Georgia, says the critics overstate the vulnerability of election systems to manipulation because they ignore the many safeguards in place. They would be better off focusing on the many sloppy software errors and poorly trained election workers that do indeed tarnish the track record of many DREs.

Still, it is worth noting that the DRE conspiracy theorists have very little to say about its close cousin, the optical scan machine in which a voter fills in a circle next to his choice and has the ballot read by a scanner. Optical scan machines present at least as many if not more security concerns because, unlike DREs, they do use a central computer. But people have employed optical scanners for decades. They are old hat and people wouldn't believe wild claims about them. New technology always carries with it the fear of the unknown; hence the "black box" label that Bev Harris has tacked onto DREs.

Despite the misplaced hysteria, it is still probably a good idea to move toward a voter-verified paper record of each ballot. Representative Rush Holt (D-NJ) has a bill to require such a paper trail for every DRE and has 106 sponsors. Representative Steve King (R-IA) has a simpler bill with fewer extraneous federal mandates for the states. Roman Buhler, a former Republican staffer for the House Administration Committee, advised King on his bill. He admits that if "Republicans can be fearful of union bosses manipulating votes in back-room boiler operations then they should sympathize if Democrats fear geeky Republican hackers in the back rooms of computer companies. The fear is mostly illegitimate, but public confidence is important."

Indeed, perception is everything. People get paper reassurance that their money is safely and accurately counted every time they use an ATM. A "voter-verified" paper trail means that, before completing the voting process, voters can examine a paper printout of their choices, under glass. This allows officials to perform a manual recount later on if there is an electronic failure.

But paper ballot records are infinitely longer than ATM receipts; they present storage problems and require heavy-duty printers that won't break down and cause chaos at a polling place. More reliable printers and new machines with verified paper trails are slowly heading for the market. However, in the November 2004 election only Nevada will have paper-trail voting machines statewide.

The price of progress is eternal vigilance about its risks. This is why it's important that we realize that DREs, along with every other new technology, can have security and accuracy problems. This doesn't mean that the technology is unworkable, but that the problems have to be squarely addressed and not swept under the rug, as some of the voting machine companies have seemed eager to do.

A Consumer's Guide to High-Tech Voting

The voting machine industry, once a sleepy backwater, has now become a hot property, with $3.9 billion in federal grants under the Help America Vote Act chasing its products. The possibility of corruption is certainly present. As *Vanity Fair* notes, "County and state officials are often softened up over lavish dinners into endorsing one kind of machine over another, with some later induced to take jobs at voting machine companies." Some of the companies also may be readier than others for the big time. Some seem to hit occasional bumps in the road, while others seem to be embarked on an interminable shakedown tour. So here is a consumer's guide to the major players.

Most of the incidents described in the following section were not fully investigated by authorities or by an independent body (which is a separate problem). So we do not have a complete explanation of why they happened. While they were caught, they raise disturbing questions that merit greater scrutiny.

DIEBOLD ELECTION SYSTEMS: The company is a division of Diebold Inc., a massive corporation that builds security systems and ATMs for a worldwide customer base in eighty-eight countries. Headquartered in Canton, Ohio, the nearly 150-year-old company reported revenue of $2.11 billion in 2003. Long before the nightmare publicity about CEO Walden O'Dell's links to Republicans, the company was in hot water.

Its trouble began in October 2003, when in the midst of California's highly controversial recall of Governor Gray Davis, Diebold election software in Alameda County malfunctioned, redistributing absentee votes to candidates they had not been cast for, including fringe candidates. So far, company officials have not explained the glitch that briefly led a Southern California socialist to victory in that county—a problem that critics claim was discovered only because there was a paper trail in the form of the physical ballots.

But the problems between Diebold and California's voters were just getting started. In December 2003, California secretary of state Kevin Shelley confronted Diebold officials after learning that the company installed uncertified software in the seventeen counties in California with electronic touch-screen voting machines. In April, Shelley asked the state's attorney general, Bill Lockyer, to consider filing criminal fraud charges against officials at Diebold. He also decertified all electronic touch-screen voting machines in the state, regardless of who made them. (Shelley later recertified some of the banned 43,000 machines for the November 2004 elections with the proviso that all-paper ballots be available for those who want them.)

Diebold's problems soon spread beyond California. In December 2003, the tireless anti-DRE journalist Bev Harris reported that individuals with criminal records had been hired at Diebold, including at least one senior vice president in charge of programming highly sophisticated election software who had been convicted and had served time for falsifying and stealing computer documents. Two other employees had criminal records—one for cocaine trafficking and the other for fraudulent stock transactions.

Three months later, in March 2004, company officials admitted that Diebold software in Alameda County had misdirected 2,747 votes in the primary for U.S. president from Senator John Kerry to Representative Dick Gephardt.

A month later, in Uxbridge, Massachusetts, Diebold machines skipped over more than 170 ballots, affecting the outcome of at least one election. Candidates in other races did not request a recount of the ballots in time, thus preventing those races from being legally recounted. One month after that, Diebold machines miscounted ballots in a close election in Marblehead, Massachusetts. The outcome in one race was supposedly 1,834 to 1,836, but a manual count showed the actual tally to be 1,831 to 1,830, overturning the election results.

Georgia had its own beef with Diebold in July 2004, when the company caused the state to violate election law by not delivering on a promise to distribute absentee ballots forty-five days before the primary election. Just twenty days before the election, in some counties, the absentee ballots had not arrived at their destinations, affecting the ability of people to vote, including American soldiers. Diebold spokesman David Bear did not have an explanation, nor could he point to who was responsible for the failure.

Diebold claims in publicity materials that it has "enjoyed years of success in the United States, Canada and Brazil," with an "unmatched" record. But critics say problems with machines owned by Diebold, and in some cases the company's employees, have caused great disruptions in several elections.

In 1998, election officials in Pima County, Arizona, found errors in the vote tally for the third time in three elections. Global Election Systems machines, sold under the Diebold name, recorded no votes in twenty-four precincts, even though voter rolls documented that thousands of people had in fact voted.

In the November 2000 presidential election, counties in Florida and New Mexico—two photo-finish states—experienced problems with Diebold machines. An internal memo leaked by whistleblowers in Diebold in 2003 (three years later) documented the disappearance of a data card in Volusia, Florida, containing 16,022 votes for Al Gore, the result of a missing card pulled from its optical scanner equipment. On election night, the Volusia votes, together with disputed returns from other counties, showed Bush with a significant winning margin. The networks, led by FOX News, began declaring Bush the winner at 2:16 on the morning after Election Day. They retracted that call two hours later when the missing votes from Volusia reappeared, but Democrats have since claimed that those missing votes played a part in the domino effect that resulted in the Bush victory.

The memos obtained from the whistleblowers indicate that Diebold did know about the problem at the time, but how it happened is apparently still a closely guarded secret inside the company.

Meanwhile, the election in New Mexico, which Al Gore won by 356 votes, was also vexed by the Diebold machines. Election officials in Bernalillo County discovered a programming flaw that led to 67,000 early voting and absentee ballots being counted incorrectly. The final results from New Mexico were delayed for almost two weeks.

In 2002, the problems with the company's software resurfaced. In Robeson County, North Carolina, a software glitch caused Diebold machines to count ballots improperly in 31 of 41 precincts. In Maryland, voters in the November 2002 election were surprised and confused when they attempted to vote for the Republican candidate for governor, and instead saw their "X" mark disappear from alongside his name and reappear next to the Democrat in the same race.

The people of Clay County, Kansas, also confronted voting irregularities brought on by Diebold voting machines, which switched the vote tallies from one candidate to another in a race for commissioner. The machines showed that the challenger won the race over the incumbent by 540 votes to 175. In reality, the results were the opposite and the incumbent won easily.

Trouble with the Diebold machines—and personnel—continued in 2003, in what had become a familiar pattern. That April, the people of Johnson County, Kansas, learned that a software error prevented votes cast at local precincts from being properly transmitted to the central counting area on election night. This led to hundreds of votes being miscounted in six precincts and necessitated a complete recount.

ADVANCED VOTING SOLUTIONS: Advanced Voting Solutions, formerly Shoup Voting Solutions, has been headed since 2001 by Howard Van Pelt, co-founder of Global Election Systems and the man who sold Global to Diebold (the election systems business is a *very* insular world).

Based in Frisco, Texas, Advanced Voting Solutions refers on its Web site to the company's "long and proud tradition in the Election Equipment and Solutions Industry," dating back to 1895, when its founders "developed the first mechanical lever machine."

Advanced Voting Solutions also boasts the only interactive wireless touch-screen voting system, which company executives say "raises the bar of the voting system technology." But some voters are convinced they can't clear the bar using the company's voting machines, which had trouble during elections in Mississippi and Virginia in 2003.

In Hinds County, Mississippi, while some computers failed to start, others broke down after overheating, leading to the complete invalidation of the local election. Officials in Fairfax, Virginia, called their election that same month a "technological and procedural failure" and said the machines' inability to record votes properly was "mind-boggling."

SEQUOIA VOTING SYSTEMS: Sequoia Voting Systems is a century-old company that produces election services and supplies as well as voting machines. The company bills itself as America's "most experienced provider of touch-screen voting systems" and the only company in the United States with an "uninterrupted track record of successful countywide installations."

Sequoia is indeed largely responsible for the nation's current interest in touch-screen voting, having pioneered the first major countywide installation in Riverside County, California, during the November 2000 election—before election reform became a national priority.

While Sequoia generally gets very high marks from election administrators, its election software has had its share of hair-pulling moments. In March 2002 in Palm Beach County, Florida, voters complained when the voting machines provided by Sequoia froze up and registered incorrect votes, which a company spokesman blamed on a programming error. One of the Palm Beach County races involved former Boca Raton mayor Emil Danciu, who claims he was ahead in the polls by seventeen points, but when the votes were tallied, he lost every precinct, even his own, receiving just under 20 percent of the vote. Numerous supporters of Danciu say they were not able to vote for him because the machines kept switching their vote to his opponent.

In another race, councilman Al Paglia, who won his primary by 45 percent against three other candidates, lost the general election by just four votes. A review of the ballots showed 78 votes registering blank, even though Paglia's race was the only one on the ballot. In addition, the system showed its vulnerability to human error when fifteen cartridges with vote information on them were discovered to be missing, only to be found at the home of a poll worker who had mistakenly brought them there.

A month later (April 2002), in Hillsborough County, Florida, there were again problems with cartridges containing votes. This time, error was due to technology, not volunteers. Votes recorded on 24 of 26 data cartridges would not transfer to be tallied and so had to be re-entered manually. The county again had trouble in March 2003 when vote counts from two more cartridges could not be transferred and also had to be re-entered manually.

In the crucial November 2002 race for governor, Sequoia client Bernalillo County, New Mexico, had more than 48,000 people show up at six sites with Sequoia voting machines. Somehow, only 36,000 were recorded. The company later admitted that voters in Clark

County, Nevada, had had the same problem with Sequoia's machines just weeks earlier.

In another county in New Mexico, which contains the town of Taos, Sequoia machines assigned votes cast to the wrong candidates in some extremely close races, including one with a 25-vote margin and another with a 79-vote lead, because of a programming error.

In November 2003, there was a power failure with one of the Sequoia machines in San Jose, California. It was repaired by unknown technicians in the middle of an election without any supervision from county officials. According to the *San Jose Mercury News*, no one on site could say what the technicians repaired or changed. Then, in March 2004, Sequoia voting machines failed to record nearly seven thousand votes in Napa County, California, because voters used the wrong ink on optical scan ballots. The glitch affected the outcome of numerous races in all levels of government as well as ballot initiative measures.

The public also learned in October 2003 that like Diebold, Sequoia had not properly protected its software codes, leaving them exposed to hackers. The software, according to Wired News, was used for storing and counting votes. In 2004, another security problem arose; this time Sequoia was criticized for its lax security by a team of university computer specialists when the company left a source code on an unsecured site. The university scientists also discovered that parts of the Sequoia system could be manipulated—specifically through Spanish-language ballots.

Sequoia has avoided some of the worst problems of other companies, but in 2001 Phil Foster, a regional vice president of Sequoia, was indicted in an alleged elections kickback scheme in Louisiana. He was accused of selling machine parts at inflated prices and of taking more than $500,000 in kickbacks. In April 2002, however, a Louisiana judge ruled that because Foster was granted immunity by Louisiana law enforcement for his testimony against others in the scheme, he could not be charged in the case. Law enforcement officials told the media that Sequoia was not involved.

HART INTERCIVIC: Based in Austin, Texas, Hart InterCivic operates in more than a dozen states. It is a new division of the Hart Company, established in 2000 to market a new voting machine, called "eslate." The company soon sold more than 26,000 eslates in twelve states, counting over four million votes. It has contracts today with such large counties as Harris County (Houston), Texas, and Orange County, California.

But Hart InterCivic has had technical problems with the eslates in both these counties. In November 2003, hundreds of would-be voters in Houston were turned away at the polls when poll workers could not get the machines to work. The eslates were not broken; rather, poll workers were not properly trained by the company to operate them.

In February 2004, in Richmond, Virginia, an eslate shut down without explanation, leaving voters to cast their votes on paper ballots. One month later, several machines shut down for about an hour at a polling place in Huntington Beach, California, causing hundreds of voters to be turned away. More trouble came just weeks later when improper training of poll workers again became a serious problem. Workers trying to run the complex voting machines in 21 districts had difficulty, resulting in more ballots cast than there were voters. In addition, election officials believe that around 5,500 voters at 55 polling locations had their ballots tabulated for the wrong location, and 1,500 additional voters used the wrong ballot altogether.

MICROVOTE GENERAL CORPORATION: Since MicroVote's founding some twenty years ago, the Indianapolis-based company says its DREs have "guaranteed the three primary requirements of any voting equipment—reliability, security, and ease of use by all voters, including those with physical restrictions."

The reliability claim is disputed by frustrated voters in Montgomery County, a suburban area bordering on Philadelphia. They saw their MicroVote system shut down numerous voting machines during the 1996 election, causing their votes to go unrecorded. Election officials learned afterward that company programmers were making changes to the voting software, which was not certified in the state, right up until the actual day of balloting.

After the election, MicroVote sued Montgomery County for $1.8 million, claiming that the malfunctions during the election were due to the county's refusal to purchase enough voting machines as promised. But a judge threw out the lawsuit. The county then sued MicroVote, among other companies involved in the election, including distributor Carson Manufacturing and the company that posted the bond, Westchester Fire Insurance. Carson settled with the county for more than $500,000, while a jury returned a verdict for the county, ordering MicroVote and Carson to pay just over $1 million in damages.

In an odd twist, Mecklenburg County (Charlotte), North Carolina, got stuck with the MicroVote machines from Montgomery when they bought them used in July 1998. The machines didn't work. County elections supervisor Bill Culp was indicted by a federal grand jury for accepting $134,000 in bribes and kickbacks from voting machine salesman Ed O'Day and repairman Gene Barnes, who had been awarded county contracts totaling millions of dollars. O'Day, an independent agent of MicroVote at the time, was convicted for bribing a government official, but landed on his feet. Today he is the vice president of the National Association of Government Suppliers.

MicroVote continued to have trouble with its machines in the November 2003 election—this time in Boone County, Indiana. The company's election software recorded 140,000 votes cast, when the county had just 50,000 residents, of whom 19,000 were registered to vote. In reality, just over 5,000 people voted, but software glitches recorded a considerably higher number.

In May 2004, in Grant County, Indiana, no votes were recorded in any precincts because of a software problem. Ironically, the problem came just weeks after Bill Carson of Carson Manufacturing, remarked in a television interview with WISH-TV how difficult and expensive it is to test voting systems. "By the time they get done testing, it [the system] is obsolete," he said. He noted that testing can cost up to ten times the cost of development. That's why election officials must insist on extensive outside auditing and parallel testing of machines *before* they buy them. The Federal Election Commission specifies numerous tests than can weed out unreliable hardware.

ELECTION SYSTEMS & SOFTWARE: We have already encountered this industry giant and the role it played in Hawaii's election fiasco of 1998. Election Systems & Software, Inc. (ES&S), headquartered in Omaha, Nebraska, is today the world's largest provider

of election systems, with 74,000 in place worldwide. It has handled over 30,000 elections in 46 states, Canada and many overseas
countries. When people go to vote in November 2004 in this country, over half of them will vote on ES&S equipment.

It began in 1980 as a startup called American International
Systems. It was founded by two brothers: Todd Urosevich, who is
a vice president of customer support for ES&S; and Bob Urosevich, now president of Diebold Election Systems, another industry giant. American International Systems got into the election
business when it did work for banks and learned that its systems
could also be sold to election officials who paid on time and
demanded much less than banks in terms of security and reliability. The company became ES&S after merging with Business
Records Corporation in 1997. ES&S is now a subsidiary of McCarthy
Group, Inc., which is jointly held by Omaha World-Herald Company, Nebraska's largest newspaper.

Aldo Tesi, president and chief executive officer of ES&S, says
the company recognizes the incredible responsibility it has to voters around the world: "We're very proud of and take seriously our
role in the democratic process. Maintaining voter confidence—
and enhancing the voting experience—is at the core of our mission as a company." However, ES&S struggles with a reputation
for both arrogance and customer dissatisfaction. An article by *Vanity Fair* alleged ES&S to be best known for its hard-charging mar-
keting efforts. "I don't understand how with the history of
performance they have—a dubious history—they can keep land-
ing big contracts," an executive at a rival company said. "They may
not be the technical choice, but they do the politics well." ES&S
spokesman Ken Fields counters with a survey of seven hundred
clients the company conducted last year, showing that 94 percent
were "satisfied or very satisfied" with ES&S equipment. But that
last 6 percent represents a lot of voters and some very close
elections.

The latest bug infestation attacked the data from optical scan
machines as well as from ES&S's iVotronic paperless voting
machines. Some of the problems: In March 2004, the voters of Indiana learned that ES&S had installed uncertified software on the
iVotronics in four counties after the certified version didn't prop-

erly and accurately count their votes. In May 2004, voters in Miami-Dade County, Florida, learned that serious bugs in ES&S software were likely to be present in all counties where ES&S was operating. The bugs caused the audit log data to fail to account for all of the ballots cast. This version also was installed in Indiana, even though the company knew about the problems, according to reports in the media and as documented on votersunite.org.

On July 9, 2004, even more bugs in the ES&S election management software were revealed in memos written by Miami-Dade election officials to ES&S. Officials told ES&S they learned that the central tabulation machines cannot handle all the audit data, have difficulty taking in data passed through phone lines, and have trouble when information that has been optically scanned is merged. Hawaii residents still remember the problems that ES&S systems experienced in their razor-thin 1998 governor's race—difficulties that I have already discussed in detail. A software programming error caused the new $3.8 million system to miss 41,015 votes on the night of the 1998 election, because the machines did not count ballots from 98 precincts. Election officials released the "final" results before realizing that one in eight votes was not counted. Tom Eschberger, a senior executive at ES&S, called the problem a "speed bump along the way" and said the votes were not lost, rather just not counted early in the process.

That same 1998 election saw glitches with ES&S machines in Rhode Island. Primary results were not released until late the next morning because of a computer glitch in the state's new $1 million system.

Two years later, in November 2000, voters in San Francisco and in Pulaski County, Arkansas, learned firsthand about the havoc that malfunctioning machines can bring. In one San Francisco polling place, 362 people signed in to vote, and 357 paper ballots were counted manually, but ES&S machines reported that 416 people had voted there. In Arkansas, nearly thirty voters reported that the machines cast their vote for the wrong candidate—after they pushed the button for their candidate of choice, another name popped up.

In April 2002, in Miami-Dade County, ES&S software changed the results of at least two city council elections, showing the real losers as the winners. Poll workers noticed the problem; ES&S machines did not give any warning. That year ES&S also had trouble spots in Wake County, North Carolina; Baldwin County, Alabama; Broward County, Florida; Sarpy County, Nebraska; Wayne County, North Carolina; Adams County, Nebraska; Lake County, Illinois; Sarasota County, Florida; and Lubbock County, Texas.

But even with its adamant denials of problems and frequent efforts to intimidate critics, the company hasn't been able to keep bad publicity away. Another incident in January 2003 garnered national attention. A special election to fill a vacant state house seat in a solidly GOP area of Broward County, Florida, featured seven Republicans and no Democrats. Over 10,000 people turned out to cast ballots, but after the tally was completed it was learned that 134 voters hadn't voted. The state house race was the *only* item on the ballot, so it seemed strange that 134 people would take the trouble to drive to the polls, walk in, sign the register, go behind the curtain and then … not vote. Since the winner captured the seat by only a twelve-vote margin, the second-place candidate was naturally concerned. The company insisted that the machine hadn't lost any votes, and it is certainly plausible that 134 Democrats who didn't know that none of their own was running showed up and then turned around in disgust. But a nagging question still remains, given how close the overall vote was.

Another headache of ES&S came in February 2002, when Arkansas secretary of state Bill McCuen pleaded guilty to accepting bribes and kickbacks from the company and not paying taxes on that money—leading to a felony conviction. Law enforcement officials say the crime involved Tom Eschberger, then an employee of Business Records Corporation, which later merged into what is now ES&S, and now the vice president at ES&S. Eschberger was granted immunity for his testimony against McCuen.

Eschberger also admitted to making campaign contributions to a potential customer in November 2003 in Louisiana in an attempt to gain business. Louisiana did hire ES&S. The voters later learned that 300 of the 900 machines from ES&S did not have shields to keep them from overheating. ES&S also showed up in Florida peddling its wares and soon landed in hot water. In 1998,

Sandra Mortham, the secretary of state before Katherine Harris, was discovered to have taken sales commissions from ES&S on sales it made inside the state after she stepped down as secretary of state. Since at the time of the sales she was also a lobbyist for the Florida Association of Counties, the customer base of ES&S, there was a clear conflict of interest. Mortham left politics under a cloud, losing a chance to be Jeb Bush's candidate for lieutenant governor.

The companies that make voting machines are correct in saying that no system can exist without a margin of error, and no one can demand perfect accuracy from it, especially if the outcome of a race isn't affected. All of the voting machine companies do good work, some more than others, but in the current climate of suspicion and even paranoia they need to do better. That's why public scrutiny of these little-known entities is called for, along with outside auditing and testing. Elections are too important now to leave in the hands of the insiders.

Where Do We Go from Here?

arsha Temple is a lawyer for the health-care group "End-of-Life Choices" in Los Angeles. Her husband, Warren Olney, hosts his own talk show on National Public Radio. Both are sophisticated observers of the political scene and active in civic affairs in Southern California.

Early this year, Marsha decided she wanted to help out the Los Angeles County registrar's office during the upcoming primary; so she volunteered to work up to four hours that day. She got a perfunctory thanks, but otherwise never heard back from the registrar until the Friday before the election, when a truck pulled up to her home near Venice Beach and unloaded several boxes containing voting machines and all the equipment needed to run a precinct.

"What is this?" Marsha asked the driver.

"It's your polling place," he replied. "You're going to be manning one all day next Tuesday in the recreation room of a nearby school."

Floored, Temple tried to call the registrar but got only a busy signal.

Knowing how short the election authorities were on volunteers—especially those under age sixty-five with sufficient stamina—Marsha resigned herself to being in charge for a fourteen-hour day rather than helping someone else for four hours, as she had planned. On election morning she and her husband drove down to the school, unloaded seven voting machines and set up shop as a polling place. Everything went smoothly, with voters drifting in and out during the day in a low turnout. At no time had Marsha heard from anyone in the registrar's office. Sometime around noon, someone from the secretary of state's office came around, poked his head inside, asked if everything was all right and then left. That was it as far as their contact with the government that day.

At the end of the day, Marsha and Warren packed up the machines, collected the ballots and prepared to drive them to the registrar's office. "I stood there and suddenly realized how vulnerable our election process is," recalls Olney. "We had hundreds of blank ballots, a signature book of voters where we could have added more names of signatures. We made a list of how we could have easily added votes that didn't exist to the totals and no one would have been the wiser. The county barely knew who we were. We realized how much we have an honor system of voting and counting in this country."

An aide in the registrar's office I spoke with admitted that Olney has a point, but said that unspecified safeguards are in place that would have prevented him from pulling off a vote heist. But apparently they were secret, because she couldn't tell me what they were. And the issue of safeguards brings us to the part of any book where an author, having identified a problem, proposes some remedies. In the past few chapters, we've seen the chaos and larceny that menace our election process. How do we restore and preserve its integrity, especially at a time when so many people have become so disenchanted with it?

The leaders in any society are unlikely to change their habits or the rules they lay down for others unless pressured to do so by the governed. If corruption exists, it is in part because we the people permit it, either by silence, by inattention or by misunderstanding. If persistent voter fraud and outdated election procedures are to be remedied, the public and the media will have to demand it. Ignoring, or refusing to recognize, the enduring problems of election fraud and mismanagement that plague many parts of our country will ensure that it spreads, mutates and grows more toxic.

"Easier to Vote, Harder to Steal"

When Congress passed the Help America Vote Act (HAVA) in 2002, its lead Democratic sponsor, Senator Chris Dodd of Connecticut, praised it for "making it easier to vote and harder to steal."

HAVA's most important reforms require that states meet two "minimum standards" in conducting their elections. One mandates that states set up a centralized, statewide voter registration list to avoid duplications and limit how often flawed voter lists prevent someone from voting. By late 2004, only about a dozen states will have completed the creation of those lists.

The other generally positive reform in HAVA is a requirement that every voter in every state be allowed to cast a "provisional" ballot if he or she shows up at a precinct and finds that his or her name is not on the registration list. For example, someone may have registered at the state DMV office while renewing a driver's license, but the DMV did not properly forward the registration application. If the authorities determine after the polls close that the voter was eligible, the vote counts.

Provisional voting can be a real safety net for someone who is the victim of a bureaucratic mistake by a local election board, something that happens all too frequently. It also means that election judges spend less time during polling hours investigating why someone isn't registered on the rolls.

But provisional voting also raises some serious concerns. The ordinary safeguards against fraud do not apply. Individuals must normally be on the voter registration lists in order to cast ballots. Allowing nonregistrants the ability to vote must be accompanied by safeguards ensuring that authorities count only legal votes. Because the federal rules on implementing provisional ballots are general, it has been left up to each state to issue detailed procedures on how to handle them.

Each state's procedures must acknowledge that HAVA specifically says that those who claim entitlement to a provisional ballot have to affirm that they are registered and eligible to vote. Provisional voting is not meant to void the registration deadlines imposed by states. While six states have same-day registration, most states have deadlines that require you to submit your registration form up to a maximum of thirty days before an election. Some voting-rights advocacy groups seem to think that as long as someone meets a residency requirement, their provisional ballot will have to be counted even if the voter never took any steps whatsoever to try to register prior to the state's deadline. These groups want to improperly use HAVA to impose same-day registration by fiat and ignore the part of the statute that requires someone to have made an effort to register. This kind of misuse of provisional voting must be discouraged.

There are also serious logistical challenges with provisional voting. Because election officials must manually search registration records for each provisional ballot, the verification and counting of provisional ballots is a major task. In 2002, when the outcome of the razor-thin Seventh District congressional race in Colorado was determined by 2,000 provisional ballots, election officials had to hire several dozen extra workers and took thirty-five days to declare a final winner. The winning margin was 121 votes, making the provisional ballots a key battleground in the post-election recount. To preserve an orderly process and have the finality of a quick decision, provisional ballots should be only for voters who need them. Otherwise, large-scale provisional balloting could disrupt Election Day procedures, creating chaos both at the polling place and in the post-election counting process.

One way that provisional ballots could easily create disorder at the polls is if voters show up at the wrong polling place and demand a provisional ballot even though they are not registered in that precinct. Some states have passed rules stipulating that votes cast outside someone's precinct will be counted for all statewide contests, but not the local ones. Other states, such as Florida, have ruled that provisional ballots cast at the wrong polling place will be discarded. Election officials in those states must be trained to direct voters to their correct precinct rather than have them cast a meaningless ballot.

In addition, there is the problem that many states are adopting the rules on how to verify provisional ballots late in this election year. In the three counties that made up the Seventh Congressional District in Colorado, one county used a provisional ballot that didn't comply with the one provided by the secretary of state's office. Matters weren't helped by the fact that the secretary of state had to issue six different rule interpretations to the counties on how they should count the ballots. One on November 7 from Bill Compton, the director of Colorado's elections division, created more panic than clarity among county election officials. It read:

> We need each of you to read between the lines on the memo regarding provisional ballots.... Please remember, SUBSTANTIAL COMPLIANCE is all that is necessary for the conduct of elections under Title One (of the Civil Rights Act). Please use your common sense and best judgment in this process.

Some states have recognized that provisional ballots are different from normal ballots and must have separate rules to ensure ballot integrity. Missouri's rules could be a model for the nation. Adopted by a Republican legislature and signed into law by a Democratic governor, Bob Holden, the rules in the "Show Me" state, not surprisingly, minimize uncertainty and ambiguity.

To cast a normal ballot in Missouri, voters must be on the registered voter list. They sign their names, verify their addresses and show some form of identification. Parties are allowed to post "challengers" at each precinct, but they cannot unduly interfere with the election process.

To cast a provisional ballot, a voter shows identification and the election judge then attempts to verify eligibility by calling the central registration office. Voters who show up at the wrong polling place are sent to the correct one. If they insist on casting a provisional ballot at the wrong location, they are given a ballot that lists only the offices such as president and governor that all voters in a state are allowed to vote on.

Missouri's experience with provisional ballots in 2002 was smooth and conflict-free. Those who had been erroneously dropped from the registration lists were allowed to vote, but the provisional ballot didn't become a vehicle for fraud. The number of provisional ballots cast wound up being only 3,603 out of a total of 1,877,620.

The concern in 2004 in other states with less well-defined rules is that outside voter-turnout groups that aren't formally affiliated with or responsible to political parties will urge people to show up at polls and vote regardless of what precinct they walk into. "It's a potential recipe for chaos, " says Robert Hess, an election law attorney in Missouri. "A precinct dominated by one party could suddenly be flooded with voters demanding provisional ballots and creating long lines for those who did follow the rules."

And, of course, if a race is close, the thousands of provisional ballots will immediately become the subject of a giant tug of war. "I'm sure in some places you will have some people demanding 'Count Every Vote,' and others who insist on the most exacting definition of who is eligible," says Bill Gardner, New Hampshire's Democratic secretary of state. That debate could be important if the number of provisional ballots represents more than the total number of votes separating the candidates on election night.

States should develop clear and unambiguous standards for how to handle and count provisional votes. The alternative is that we might have a Florida-style dispute spilling into the courts in several states where the presidential race is close, with one side calling for all provisional ballots to be tabulated ("Count Every Vote") and the other demanding that the law be scrupulously observed. In the absence of clear rules, we can expect lawyers to try and turn the most implausible legal theory into a court ruling in their favor. Vague rules on provisional voting could create a nightmare in which the results of the presidential race aren't known for days. Recall the thirty-five days it took Colorado officials to decide one congressional race.

A Question of Identity

The most often discussed proposal to limit fraud and irregularities at the polls is a requirement that all voters show photo ID before voting, much as they now do when they take an airline flight, buy an Amtrak ticket, cash a check, rent a video or check into a hotel. Poll after poll shows the concept is popular and easily understood by the American people. A Rasmussen Research poll taken for this book found that 82 percent of Americans believed voters should show photo ID. The majorities included 89 percent of Bush voters and 75 percent of both Kerry voters and those who described themselves as liberals.

Yet this is one of the most bitterly fought reforms. Civil rights groups delayed a vote on the Help America Vote Act of 2002 because a single provision required states to ask first-time voters who registered by mail to show identification at the polls. HAVA finally passed into law in October 2002, a full two years after the Florida debacle, meaning that it will be only partially implemented in the 2004 elections.

Even though the photo ID requirement applies to only a very small number of voters, groups such as the NAACP and La Raza Unida claim it is the equivalent of a modern poll tax, a barrier to voting that discriminates against voters who are easily intimidated such as the elderly, non-English speakers and the poor, many of whom have no driver's license. "In November 2004, there is every reason to believe a significant number of eligible voters will be turned away on ID grounds, perhaps enough to decide a close election," the *New York Times* editorialized in the spring of 2004.

Opposition to photo ID laws has often reached comical levels. In the 1990s, the Clinton administration managed to come up with a public policy argument that people had to show a photo ID to buy cigarettes, while on the other hand, a state could not fight election fraud by requiring photo ID. The circus began in February 1997 when the Clinton Food and Drug Administration issued decrees against teen smoking, which ordered all stores that sell tobacco to demand photo ID from everyone who looks to be twenty-seven years or younger. At the same time, the Clinton Justice Department contended that Louisiana was out of bounds in asking adult voters to prove they really were who they said they were.

The Justice Department position was ironic given that Louisiana had just gone through a fresh voter fraud scandal. In the spring of 1997, the U.S. Senate was investigating allegations that the 1996 skin-tight election of Democrat Mary Landrieu to a Senate seat was hopelessly tainted by thousands of phantom votes, including 1,380 people registered at abandoned buildings. A New Orleans assistant city attorney has resigned in protest over election irregularities in the Landrieu race, and Morris Reed, a judge and unsuccessful black candidate for city attorney, was also charging election fraud in New Orleans.

State legislators in Louisiana had recognized that their state had to clean up its act even before the Landrieu election, back in 1994, after the *Lake Charles American Press* decided to test the system by sending twenty-five fictitious applications signed only with an "X" to eight different voter registrars. Twenty-one were approved and put on the rolls, an 80 percent success rate in cheating. Eye-popping examples such as this prompted Louisiana's legislature, led by state senator (later governor) Mike Foster, to require that mail-in registrant voters show photo identification, though only when they voted for the first time.

But Louisiana was one of the states required by the Voting Rights Act to "pre-clear" changes in its election laws with the U.S. Justice Department. Justice threw out the ID provision on grounds that fewer black voters hold driver's licenses than do white people. Justice also claimed that the Louisiana law imposed a more restrictive ID requirement on voters who register by mail. After much public ridicule over its contradictory stance regarding cigarette buyers, Justice finally dropped its objections to the Louisiana photo ID law.

In the seventeen states that now also require *all* voters to present some form of documentation at the polls, ample provision is made for voters without a driver's license. Other acceptable forms of identification include the photo ID that driver's license bureaus issue to nondrivers, a utility bill, a paycheck, military ID or any other piece of information that might include a picture, date of birth, home address or signature. Those who lack the acceptable ID must in every state be allowed to sign an affidavit and cast a provisional ballot that is counted later, after the voter's eligibility is confirmed.

Many more states have considered a photo ID requirement for all voters since the 2000 Florida debacle. Legislatures in New Hampshire, Wisconsin, Iowa, Arizona and Kansas passed such laws only to see Democratic governors veto them. In Kansas, the Democratic state senate minority leader, Anthony Hensley, went so far as to call the law "a solution in search of a problem" because no evidence of voter fraud existed.

But some states did finally agree on a compromise after heated debate. In Mississippi, a state with bad memories of civil rights workers being murdered for registering blacks, the debate over a photo ID bill was at first incendiary. State senator David Jordan, a Democrat from Greenwood, called the idea "rotten from the core. It is evil. It is wrong.... This is a back door to a poll tax." Another senator recalled the days when dogs in his Delta hometown were set loose on African Americans trying to vote. But the Mississippi Senate passed the bill in February 2004 after amending it to add penalties, among them a $1,000 fine, for anyone utilizing voter ID for the purpose of intimidation. In the state house, the bill was further amended to exempt those over age sixty-five, the assumption being that they would be the only people to have painful memories of having been denied the right to vote in the 1960s. The final bill was approved 92 to 28, although only ten black members voted in favor.

Same-Day Registration

The other most talked about reform of the election system—which is not a reform at all but an added opportunity for mischief—comes from those who believe it is vitally important we make sure as many people as possible vote. Their favorite reform is same-day voter registration, which would allow new voters to register on Election Day. It is now used in Wisconsin, Minnesota and four other states.

In 2002, two liberal millionaires put the idea on state ballots in California and Colorado. They argued that registration deadlines of fifteen days before Election Day in California and thirty days in Colorado prevented some people from voting. Their proposals would have allowed anyone to show up at the polls, present a driver's license or some other document with his name and address on it, register on the spot and vote.

State and local election officials were generally opposed. Colorado secretary of state Donetta Davidson said the program would prevent counties from checking for fraud and require her to train thousands of poll workers to handle new computer equipment that would be required. In California, Connie McCormack, the voter registrar of Los Angeles County, warned that "Elections are in danger of collapsing under the weight of their own complexity." Other registrars opposed Proposition 52, as the same-day registration idea was identified, because it would not require "provisional ballots" for those who register on Election Day. (Current law requires that people whose eligibility is in dispute have their ballots separated and verified later.)

If the initiative had passed, voters who registered on Election Day would have had their ballots mixed in with everyone else's. If investigators later proved there was fraud, there would be no way to know who was responsible. An aide to California secretary of state Bill Jones warned that under Proposition 52, busloads of people could "move into" a close, targeted district for a day and vote, then leave town, without technically breaking the law.

Minnesota secretary of state Mary Kiffmeyer also admitted she was tired of hearing her state's same-day registration extolled. She compares it to holding a party and not knowing how much food to buy because no one sent in an RSVP. Some precincts run out of ballots, while others are overstocked. "We have long lines because of same-day," she says. "People get frustrated and leave."

The states that have tried same-day registration are mostly small, with stable populations and long traditions of good government. Even so, problems crop up. In 1986, Oregon voters overwhelmingly scrapped the idea after a cult that wanted to take over a town government tried to register hundreds of supporters on Election Day. In 2000, a New York socialite working for Al Gore scandalized Wisconsin when a TV camera caught her bribing street vagrants with packs of cigarettes if they went to the polls. She pleaded guilty to fraud. At Marquette University in Milwaukee, 174 students boasted that they had voted more than once. They quickly changed their story when prosecutors pointed out that voting twice is a crime. Also that year, the U.S. Postal Service returned at least 3,500 Election Day registration confirmations as undeliverable in Wisconsin—meaning that thousands of people had registered to vote and probably cast ballots with the wrong address on Election Day. For what it's worth, Al Gore won Wisconsin by 5,700 votes.

Even some supporters of Election Day registration in smaller states quail when asked about its use in America's most populous state. Curtis Gans, director of the Committee for the Study of the

American Electorate, says the risk of fraud in California is too great. "It's not beyond the imagination that one party or another will register aliens on the last day," he said. "And there's no protection against that except criminal penalties, which have not been effective."

Proponents of same-day voter registration spent millions in both California and Colorado promoting their initiative. But liberal newspapers shrank from the idea, with the *San Francisco Chronicle*, the *Los Angeles Times* and the *Denver Post* all editorializing against it. Even California's liberal governor Gray Davis opposed the idea. "His view is that voters who go to the polls ought to have a minimum amount of information about what they are voting on," explained Davis aide Garry South. On Election Day, same-day registration lost 59 to 41 percent in California, trailing in 45 out of 53 congressional districts. In Colorado, it won less than 40 percent of the vote, losing even liberal strongholds such as Denver and Boulder.

Same-day registration is the latest gimmick dreamed up by people who say they want to boost voter turnout. We've been down this road before. The Motor Voter Law allows people to register to vote at the Department of Motor Vehicles. Liberal absentee voter laws let people cast ballots while on vacation or from remote locations. And some states allow for early voting—casting a ballot before Election Day. All these provisions have failed to increase voter turnout. It's about time that someone stepped forward and admitted that the root cause of low turnout isn't restrictive voting laws, but voter apathy. Some people are fed up with mediocre candidates, gerrymandered districts and uncompetitive (and possibly illegitimate) elections.

Rein in Voter-Chasing Lawyers

If we don't invest in better election procedures, equipment and voter education, we may pay for our failure by turning Election Day into Election Month through a new legal quagmire: election by litigation. "After Florida in 2000, election night is not necessarily the finish line anymore," says Doug Chapin, who runs Electionline.org, a clearinghouse of voting information. "Both sides are lawyering up to hit the ground running if anything happens."

Something is guaranteed to happen. You can bet that in a country with 170,000 polling places, some disputes are inevitable. Around 25 percent of American voters will be using controversial new electronic voting machines that will become a magnet for lawsuits. Many other Americans will still use the same punch-card voting machines that resulted in so much confusion in Florida's 2000 election, and could lead to new disputes this time in states with close contests.

There are clear signs that the warring camps are going to see each other in court. In July, John Kerry announced the creation of a nationwide legal SWAT team of election lawyers to take "tough action" against the voter "intimidation and harassment" that he claims kept 57,000 African Americans in Florida from the polls in 2000.

But specific, hard evidence for that claim involving real people has been elusive. In Florida, the civil rights coalition monitoring voting says it has "no confidence" in the Justice Department because it "refused to act" on the evidence of "massive voter disenfranchisement" in the 2000 election. But if Attorney General Janet Reno, a Democrat who knows Florida well, didn't find such evidence in the ten weeks after the 2000 election when she investigated the matter, one wonders what facts Mr. Kerry is referring to.

For their part, Republicans are conducting training sessions to respond to complaints of absentee ballot fraud, duplicate registrations and elderly residents of nursing homes being overly "assisted" in marking their ballots. They promise to have lawyers monitoring as many as 30,000 precincts or about one-sixth of the country. GOP lawyers also fear that in a close election, Democratic lawyers will take advantage of a flood of provisional ballots cast by people who aren't on the voter registration rolls and demand that all of them be counted regardless of eligibility, reprising the "Count Every Vote!" chant from Florida.

Democrats, who scoff that GOP concerns about election fraud are a cover for attempts to intimidate voters, are certain to outgun the Republicans in the legal arms race this fall. One reason is the ecstatic response of trial lawyers to the presence of John Edwards on the Democratic ticket. Fred Baron, a former president of the

Association of Trial Lawyers of America, is a top fundraiser for the Kerry-Edwards ticket.

In 2002, ATLA became the largest single contributor to federal candidates, almost exclusively to Democrats. They are an even more important ally of the Democratic Party in 2004, as evidenced by the presence of Mr. Edwards on the ticket. The 2000 Florida recount also allowed trial lawyers to make the argument to Democrats that lawyers could be as important as voters in determining elections and they should invest heavily in legal muscle. The trial lawyers have an enormous stake in Democratic victories in 2004. This year alone, the Senate only narrowly blocked efforts by the Bush White House to rein in class-action lawsuits and limit liability in asbestos-related claims.

In 2002, trial lawyers were extremely active in Democratic efforts to prepare for post-election litigation. Lance Block, former president of the Academy of Florida Trial Lawyers, boasted that his office was "ground zero" for the deployment of Democratic lawyers to polling places. In Colorado, a Democratic request to the Colorado Trial Lawyers Association for pro bono election help was swiftly forwarded to all its members.

Similar e-mail requests for trial lawyer volunteers to help prepare cookie-cutter lawsuits to be filed before the election were sent out in the summer of 2004. In the fall election, you can expect lots of lawyers from both parties to be monitoring the polls. Some even plan to wear signs around their neck so voters with a problem can turn to a voter-chasing lawyer on the spot.

Last month, as I previously mentioned, thirteen Democrats from the U.S. House of Representatives wrote a letter to U.N. Secretary-General Kofi Annan asking him to send "election monitors" to observe this fall's U.S. election. Annan, consumed with his own embezzlement scandal, wisely declined to get involved. But that doesn't mean monitors wouldn't necessarily be a bad thing. For example, who will monitor the lawyers as they turn American politics into another breeding ground for endless litigation?

Vanishing Volunteers

America has a vanishing corps of Election Day poll workers, as
elderly workers retire or die and it becomes increasingly difficult
to convince younger generations to take on a job that involves fourteen-hour days without a break and pays between $65 and $120
for a long day of work. Increasingly, the complexity of election
laws has made the job stressful and added the possibility of verbal or other abuse from angry voters. There is also the possibility
of election workers being sent on wild-goose chases. Carol Anne
Coryell, the former nonpartisan election administrator of Fairfax
County, Virginia, recalls that during the 2000 presidential election
she was constantly getting complaints from Democratic lawyers
about voters being disfranchised. "It got to the point where I would
almost call it harassment," she says. "I checked with both the Democratic and Republican election official at every precinct where there
were reports of people not being able to vote, denied the right to
vote, and even people having to recite their Social Security number in public. None, I mean none, checked out. They took me away
from real problems I should have dealt with."

"The lack of poll workers is a huge problem across the nation,
and it's only going to get worse if states and counties don't act
quickly," says Kay Albowicz of the National Association of Secretaries of State. "When the current crop gets to where they can't
stand the long days, there's probably not going to be very many
people to replace them."

The shortage of poll workers is already affecting the integrity
of some elections. In March 2002, an unprecedented number of
polling-place workers didn't report for work in Los Angeles County.
A total of 124 precincts opened late and one didn't open at all. Now
registrar Connie McCormack increasingly has to use county workers who get their regular pay for eight hours, but no overtime. She
and other election officials know that's not a long-term solution.

Most of the election officials I interviewed estimated that the
average age of their poll workers was in the late sixties. But with
the increasing importance of technology in the election process,
there is a greater need than ever for the technical talents of young
people.

Some efforts are under way that would turn college students and graduating seniors in high school into poll workers. The Help America Vote Foundation is working with states to change laws that require poll workers to be over eighteen and also registered voters. Their hope is that young people who work at the polls as understudies to older poll workers may become engaged enough to want to help out after they leave school.

Students who aren't up to being full-fledged poll workers could also help. The technologically savvy can explain the voting machines to those who need an explanation. They can help new and elderly voters understand the process. They can assist disabled voters who need help to get to the polling place. Some can even serve as translators.

Compounding the challenge of involving young people in the election process is the fact that in many schools, civics is no longer part of the curriculum. In his Farewell Address as he left the presidency in 1989, Ronald Reagan warned of the consequences of not educating Americans in their history. "If we forget what we did, we won't know who we are," he said. "I am warning of an eradication of the American memory that could result, ultimately, in an erosion of the American spirit. Let's start with some basics: more attention to American history and a greater emphasis on civic ritual."

Few would argue that since 1989 we have paid enough attention to Reagan's warning. We may be paying part of the price for that every election cycle, when it becomes harder and harder to find enough poll workers. A shorthanded election process will eventually become a process that shortchanges the people.

Absent Rules, Enter Fraud

Absentee ballots represent the biggest source of potential election fraud because of the way they are obtained and voted. "All of us know that absentee voting is our least well protected part of the election process," says Doug Lewis, executive director of the Election Center, a Houston-based clearinghouse for the National Association of State Election Directors. Some simple steps would make it more difficult to abuse absentee ballots.

The envelope that an absentee ballot is placed in should be signed by the voter in the presence of at least one witness whose address and phone number are provided. Only the voter should be allowed to request an absentee ballot, not the voter's family members, because such a procedure makes it impossible to compare the signature on a request form with the voter's signature file. Third parties such as campaign workers should be barred from delivering absentee ballots. This would prevent the alteration of ballots by campaign organizations and others.

States should be required to run computer comparisons on a regular basis to match their voter lists with death records and corrections department files to delete deceased individuals and felons who are ineligible to vote. Currently, the procedures in most states are inadequate and slow.

Federal immigration officials should also change their administrative procedures to allow immigration data to be used by local election officials to better police the voter registration rolls. During a bitter recount of an Orange County congressional race in 1996, the California secretary of state found that in just one five-month period a minimum of 125 registered voters had declined to serve on juries because they were noncitizens. Cases were turned over to local prosecutors, but no charges were filed.

State election authorities should be authorized to establish a national central death registry that would collect information on all deaths from state vital records agencies and provide each state with the information needed to purge deceased voters. Even states that have good record-keeping systems do not receive data on registered voters who have died outside the state. A central death registry would allow election authorities to check for multiple registrations.

State officials such as secretaries of state should also be granted investigative subpoena powers to look into both voter fraud and disfranchisement issues. Historically, election officials have relied too heavily on candidates to identify election problems. Most election boards do not have the authority to conduct vigorous investigations of voter fraud and must rely on local district attorney's offices that are usually heavily engaged in criminal cases and not interested in prosecuting election fraud for fear of being labeled partisan or racially motivated. Election officials should have the investigative powers necessary to pursue cases and to impose administrative fines on violators. Similarly, state attorneys general should be authorized to use statewide grand juries to investigate election fraud anywhere in a state.

Local registration and election boards should be composed of citizen appointees. All such boards should have equal representation from both major political parties and at least one independent or third-party member. We've seen over and over, from St. Louis to Palm Beach County, how conflicts of interest are created if election boards are run by officials who have to run for offices themselves—often as partisans. "I think you'll see most of the problems in bad management of elections occur where the top position isn't nonpartisan and where most of the oversight is by people deeply involved in the political process," says Mischelle Townsend, the registrar of voters in Riverside County, California.

All county and municipal election authorities should be required to have independent audits conducted of their voter tabulation systems, software and security procedures on a regular basis. In business, companies undergo outside audits by independent bodies to confirm to their stockholders that the companies are truthfully reporting on their financial condition and status. Election bodies should also be required to have outside audits to confirm to their stockholders, the voting public, that their security procedures are sufficient to guarantee free and fair elections.

Independent, nonpartisan groups, as well as candidates and parties, should be authorized to appoint poll watchers to observe the election and vote tabulation process. Poll watchers are essential for running elections that are free of fraud and manipulation. In addition to having poll watchers in specific precincts, parties, candidates and nonpartisan groups should be able to designate statewide poll watchers with authority to observe activities at any precinct or vote tabulation center.

All vendors who supply voting machines and computer software programs should be required to undergo investigation by competent bodies of the financial solvency, security and integrity of the vendor. Most states have no such requirement for election vendors. Only an investigation similar to the one that lottery vendors must undergo in most states can ensure that election machine manufacturers have a good track record in other jurisdictions and won't manipulate voting results.

Decisions on which ballot counting technologies to use should remain at the state and local level. However, we should phase out "central counting stations" where punch cards, touch-screen or optical-scan ballots are tabulated, often requiring the ballots to be moved from one location to another before being counted. Far more spoiled ballots turn up at these central stations than at individual polling sites, because voters cannot be notified of their errors if the ballots have been moved.

We should take seriously concerns about poor election administration in racial minority neighborhoods. Even though the claims by the U.S. Commission on Civil Rights that there were conscious attempts to intimidate minority voters in Florida in 2000 were baseless, the commission did identify concerns that many minority voters have about the system. These have been bolstered by recent polls showing that some one out of seven minority voters don't believe their ballots are counted correctly. At the same time, we should not let charges of racism distract us from the push for reform. A study by University of Missouri political scientists Martha Kropf and Steven Knack found that African Americans live disproportionately in counties with *more* reliable voting technology. Antiquated equipment is largely located in counties with white and Republican majorities.

Clear and consistent rules for identifying what constitutes a vote and for the timetables and procedures for contesting an election result must be developed by each state. Disputes over the vagueness in Florida's election law inflamed the controversial 2000 recount in Florida. The Supreme Court in *Bush v. Gore* stated that voters in states should be given "equal protection of the law" in assuring that all votes are counted equally, but also held that its ruling wouldn't be a precedent in other cases. Establishing the legitimacy of a vote is a tricky business. Overvotes, for two or more candidates, and undervotes, for no candidate, can have very different meanings. Overvotes are usually the result of a mistake, but about 70 percent of undervotes are deliberate because a voter chose not to make a decision.

Honoring Our Troops

The federal government should undertake to ensure that states handle military ballots in a fair and expedited manner. As E. J. Dionne of the *Washington Post* put it, "Absentee ballots from service members overseas need to be treated with the utmost care and subjected to ballot-counting criteria that are, at a minimum, no more stringent than those applied to regular ballots."

The problem is real. A substantial minority, perhaps 40 percent or more, of those military personnel who try to vote by submitting completed Federal Post Card Applications are unable to do so because of overly complicated overseas absentee voting procedures and, most importantly, inadequate ballot transmission time. (Military personnel almost always use the FPCA to apply for absentee ballots because this federal form is available from military voting assistance officers and because federal law requires all states to accept the form.)

The only state for which we have statewide data is Missouri. Secretary of State Matt Blunt is so far the only state election official to send a questionnaire to local officials asking for a report on how military ballots are handled. Blunt has a real interest in the issue as a lieutenant commander in the Naval Reserve. After 9/11, he was recalled to active duty and sent outside the United States for several months, the only statewide elected official so called to active duty.

Secretary Blunt distributed the questionnaire to Missouri's 116 local election officials and received responses from 105 of them. (The City of St. Louis was one of the holdouts.) Those 105 election officials reported receiving 1,147 completed post card applications for ballots in the 2002 general election. No doubt some ballots were sent out and not returned; we will never know that number. We do know that only 673 of those applicants (58.7 percent) ended up casting ballots that were counted. Clearly, many other ballots were either lost or disqualified—a situation we should remedy.

The problem is that most states are still conducting absentee voting essentially as they did in World War II, depending upon snail mail for all three steps: the transmission of the absentee ballot request from the voter to the election official, the transmission of the unmarked ballot from the election official to the voter, and the transmission of the marked ballot from the voter to the election official. Each of these steps can take weeks if the mail must be used, but only seconds if secure electronic means were authorized.

Early in 2004, the Department of Defense canceled the Secure Electronic Registration and Voting Experiment (SERVE), after spending $25 million on this project to enable 100,000 military personnel and family members to vote electronically in the 2004 general election. Defense canceled SERVE because of legitimate security concerns, but some substitute program should be instituted to make it possible for military personnel to vote with reasonable assurance that their ballots will be counted. I favor a system that is two-thirds electronic: the service member should be able to make an electronic application for an absentee ballot, and the election official should be able to transmit the unmarked ballot to the military voter by electronic means. Then, the voter could print out the ballot and the required affidavit and return envelope. Until we have greater confidence in the technology, we should require all absentee voters to return their marked ballots by U.S. mail or a commercial delivery service like DHL or Federal Express. At least one of those companies is interested in carrying military ballots under a contract that would charge a pittance of the normal shipping charges.

Federal Bureaucrat Runs Amok

One of the more bizarre election stories of 2004 occurred in July, when one of the most controversial figures in the Bush administration—DeForest B. Soaries, chairman of the newly created Federal Election Assistance Commission—wrote to Homeland Security secretary Tom Ridge and asked him to seek an emergency law from Congress giving the FEAC "authority to cancel and reschedule a federal election" in the wake of a terrorist attack. Secretary Ridge forwarded the Soaries letter to the Justice Department for review, but made it clear that he didn't agree with all of the conclusions in it. Mr. Soaries put it more bluntly. "What Ridge basically said is, 'I don't have time to meet with you,'" he told the Associated

Press. "I'm still assuming that there's time for us to meet to share information and work cooperatively on all of these important issues."

Soaries' comments, coming from an election agency that is primarily concerned with distributing federal grants to improve voting standards, struck many as a classic case of Washington bureaucratic hubris. A Democratic House aide said that despite good intentions, "what's all this stirring the pot going to get us right now, except for scaring people away from the polls?"

Soaries is a minister who ran for Congress as a Republican in New Jersey in 2002. He is known for inspirational speeches and a keen desire to expand his bureaucratic sandbox. With the Constitution stipulating that states and localities control the "time, manner and place" of elections, FEAC has been restricted to providing states and localities with election advice and grants, along with setting some basic standards. But Mr. Soaries seems to want more. "We have a federal election without federal involvement," he complains. "With 200,000 precincts in the country there's a lot of room for variance." Sounds as if Rev. Soaries thinks the feds ought to "solve" that problem. He recently gave an entire speech on FEAC voting standards for the states without even once mentioning the word "voluntary." Now he wants his baby agency to have the power to cancel and reschedule national elections, something that was never done during the Civil War or either of two World Wars.

At least the Soaries flap had one silver lining. His intervention started several people worrying that the FEAC might in the future morph into a new Federal Election Commission by acquiring more rule-making powers that would allow it to affect the outcome of a close election. Under current rules, the FEAC could also become biased in a partisan direction if an unscrupulous president decided to stack it with his own party's members through recess appointments just before an election. Before the FEAC grows even more prone to insert itself into areas where it has no mandate, Congress should set clear limits for its reach when the commission comes up for reauthorization next year.

The Road Ahead

Many Americans still smart from a history of discriminatory hurdles to voting, and instinctively resist anything that smacks of exclusion. That is understandable. We should oppose any attempt to create artificial barriers to voter participation.

Discrimination can take many forms: turning away voters already in line when polls close, intimidating or misinforming voters when they arrive at the polls, using badly flawed or poorly designed ballots, failing to provide bilingual materials and failing to fix problem voting machines. We must guard against all these practices. But we also must recognize that voters have a responsibility to acquaint themselves with the election process and they cannot expect that their vote will be counted no matter what mistakes they make in casting it. Better voter education in schools, literacy programs and public service announcements before an election reminding people what they must do to cast a valid vote can all help reduce the number of spoiled ballots and ensure that as many valid votes as possible are cast.

We also should consider paying the people who run our elections more, as well as giving some of them more professional training. We pay many of the election officials in some of our rural counties less than the janitors at the local school. Sue Woody, who had served as the clerk of Park County, Indiana, resigned last year because she couldn't make it on her salary of $22,000. She was responsible for running both the court and the election systems for her county.

But we also have to return to the traditional view that citizenship requires orderly, clear and vigorous procedures to ensure that the integrity of our elections is maintained. An era of rampant sloppiness has influenced the election process to the point where opportunists or enthusiasts can take advantage of casual "inclusive" rules to alter the course of public affairs. "The more rules are settled in advance, the better elections we will have," says Brad King, a former state elections director of Minnesota, who is the new co-director of Indiana's elections division. "What we don't want is the designed sloppiness that a few politicians allow to seep into our system through ambiguity and vagueness." Ambiguity in election law is a surefire recipe for funny business at the polls, litigation and a chance that some votes won't be counted properly.

But few in the media or urban governments seem concerned about the designed sloppiness of our election system. There is also an increasing brazenness by many people who want their side to cut corners if it helps them win. Filmmaker Michael Moore is free to make *Fahrenheit 9/11* in a direct attempt to defeat George W. Bush. But he is not supposed to use his celebrity status to make light of bribing people to vote. In the "Do Something" section of his Web site he suggests that supporters of John Kerry "offer a six-pack to anyone in the office who votes (make sure you're not working in cubicles full of Republicans!) . . . Promise to have sex with a non-voter—whatever it takes!"

Moore also stands accused of doctoring a newspaper headline shown in *Fahrenheit 9/11*. Given that every media examination of the 2000 election in Florida found that George W. Bush would have won a statewide recount, Moore was obviously hard up for headlines that would bolster his claim that the Bush forces had stolen the election. He wound up using one from *The Pantagraph*, a newspaper in Bloomington, Illinois. In the film, a copy of the paper's front page from December 19, 2001, is reproduced with the headline: "Latest Florida recount shows Gore won election." The only problem is that *The Pantagraph*'s editors say those words didn't run in its December 19 edition, but rather on December 5 and not on the front page. Instead, the headline appeared in much smaller type above a letter to the editor, which the paper says reflects "only the opinions of the letter writer." The falsification of historical evidence here is calculated and blatant, and the paper is understandably demanding an apology. Given Moore's track record of "hit and run" journalism, however, the paper's editors can expect to wait a long time. And few in the media have called Moore on his deception.

Our current lax enforcement of voting laws, in which prosecutors shy away from bringing election fraud cases unless the evidence is almost literally handed to them on videotape, is analogous to having counterfeit bills circulating and the Treasury not wanting to be bothered until the printing press is located.

Should "anything goes" continue to be ballot bywords, the nation may wake to another crisis even bigger than the 2000 Florida folly. Perhaps then it will demand to know who subverted the safeguards in its election laws. But wouldn't it be better if—with the lessons of Florida still fresh in the minds of many people—we did something now?

Acknowledgments

xpressing appreciation to those who helped make a book possible is always a tricky endeavor. You are almost certain to forget someone, so apologies are offered in advance to anyone whom I inadvertently pass over.

This book would never have been possible if I didn't have the opportunity to work at the editorial page of the *Wall Street Journal*, the most congenial and supportive workplace imaginable for someone who wants to examine and comment on issues of the day. Robert Bartley, the late editor of the *Journal*, was convinced early on that voter fraud would be a growing problem, and he and his deputy, Dan Henninger, allowed me to spend an inordinate amount of time delving into the topic. Their interest was sustained and broadened by Paul Gigot, the current editor, who knows a good story when he sees so much of the rest of the media ignoring something. James Taranto and Brendan Miniter vastly improved many of the articles I wrote for the *Journal*'s Web site, OpinonJournal. Some sections of this book are drawn in part from material previously published in the *Wall Street Journal* and on OpinionJournal.

I am especially grateful to Peter Collier of Encounter Books for believing in this project. He and his staff pulled off amazing feats of speed and vigor in getting this to readers before the 2004 election. I appreciate the help of Carol Staswick for copyediting and for making all the pieces fit just so. The book benefited from having excellent public relations counsel from Amy Packard, Kay Daly and Tom Lipscomb. Martin Wooster stepped in to do some critical research; any author would benefit from his meticulous combing of libraries.

I am in debt to friends in the think tank and philanthropic world who provided helpful advice, including John Samples of the Cato Institute, Ed Feulner of the Heritage Foundation, John Raisian at the Hoover Institution and Jim Piereson of the John M. Olin Foundation.

This book was born out of a conversation I had over dinner with several friends at Ellis Alden's splendid vineyard in the Alexander Valley of California. I am only sorry I could not take Ellis up on his kind offer to let me write some of this book at the place where the inspiration for it came.

Many chapters were improved by conversations with the late Joe Beard, Brenda Burns, Glenn Simpson, Linda Morrison, Cathy McMorris, Gay and Stanley Gaines, Dan Walters, John Barnes, Heather and James Higgins, Grover Norquist, Damon Ansell, Mallory Factor, Jim Lucier, Darcy Olsen, Sal Russo, Jon Caldera and David Biddulph. Melissa Hart made connections for me in Pennsylvania that I couldn't otherwise have made. Melanie Morgan and Grant Gillham provided useful insight on my home state of California, which I admit I can't follow as closely as I would want from across the country. My brother Bob in Arizona and my sister Sue in Oregon did the same for two other hotspots of election trouble.

Gail Heriot was a stalwart supporter of this project from the very beginning and made invaluable suggestions. I will always be grateful to Clara del Villar for her encouragement. Democrats such as Paul Goldman, former Virginia governor Doug Wilder, the late congressman Ned Pattison, Karen Saranita, Melody Rose and former Philadelphia city councilman James Tayoun offered indispensable help in separating serious voting problems from partisan complaints. Martha Montelongo and Tunku Varadarajan provided me with perspectives on voting and ballot security from outside my culture. And, of course, I owe my parents more than I can ever say.

Notes

Introduction

page
1   "at least eight of the nineteen hijackers": Interview with Michael Chertoff, head of the Justice Department's Criminal Division, December 22, 2002.

2   "a Rasmussen Research poll": Survey of 1,500 likely voters, June 11–13, 2004.

3   "John Kerry campaigned in Florida": FOX News transcript, April 19, 2004.

5   "This system was instrumental": Interview with President Vicente Fox, March 11, 2001.

6   "Earl Mazo, the journalist who exhaustively": Peter Baker, *Washington Post*, November 11, 2000.

8   "The U.S. attorney for the Northern District of Louisiana": *Shreveport Times*, August 31, 2003.

Chapter One

11   "Zogby found that": *Houston Chronicle*, July 9, 2000.

12   " 'Then one of the workers brought out' ": Interview with John Zogby, July 9, 2004.

13   "McAuliffe wrote back to say": Letter posted on Web site of Democratic National Committee's Voting Rights Institute, July 2, 2004.

15   "city attorney Louise Renne": Interview on KCBS Radio, July 10, 2004.

15   "carried a brochure": Florida Department of Law Enforcement Report on Voter Fraud, January 1998.

17   "'If I erred in doing so'": *Indian Country Today*, November 4, 2002.

19   "The subject remains a sensitive one": Interview with David Keene, June 9, 2004.

20   "But the most well-publicized incident": Interview with Donna Brazile, September 10, 2003.

22   "Horrocks had contempt for Allen": Interview with Francis Allen, May 11, 2004.

24   "Gans believes that": Interview with Curtis Gans, July 8, 2004.

Chapter Two

29   "Kirsanow says that": *National Review*, July 12, 2004.

30   "Lott found that": U.S. Commission on Civil Rights, Minority Report, August 2001.

32   "'These illegal voters'": *Palm Beach Post*, May 28, 2001.

38   "Despite appeals from Lott": Interview with John Lott, June 21, 2004.

39   "But more than 3,000 voters": Interview with Theresa LePore, December 4, 2000.

Chapter Three

41   "Today, twenty-six states": Final Report of the National Conference of State Legislatures Elections Reform Task Force, September 2001.

44   "Author Elizabeth Drew": Elizabeth Drew, *Whatever It Takes: The Real Struggle for Political Power in America* (Viking, 1997).

44   "It argued that these methods": Forum on Election Reform, "Building Consensus on Election Reform," 2001, p. 14.

47   "Robert Jambois, the Kenosha County": *Wall Street Journal*, October 25, 2002.

49   "There was good reason to change": Interview with former Florida secretary of state Jim Smith, December 1, 2000.

49   "One Michael Yip": *Miami Herald*, February 1, 1998.

50   "It is the part of California": *Almanac of American Politics, 2004*.

51   "Mary Torres of Bakersfield": E-mail message, November 20, 2002.

52   "She says it hasn't raised": Interview with Melody Rose, October 3, 2002.

54 "'Anytime you have more paper ballots'": Interview with New Hampshire secretary of state Bill Gardner, February 19, 2004.

Chapter Four

57 "'Hey, stay for the election'": Steve Hilton, *St. Louis Post-Dispatch*, March 28, 2002.

59 "Not that Judge Baker": Bill McClellan, *St. Louis Post-Dispatch*, November 12, 2000.

62 "But Dowd never told Baker": *Insight* magazine, July 16, 2001.

62 "Some of the orders were clearly": *St. Louis Post-Dispatch*, December 5, 2000.

64 "Secretary Blunt's investigation": Missouri Secretary of State's Report on Conduct of Election in City of St. Louis, May 2001.

65 "In March 2002 he focused": Interview with Senator Kit Bond, June 17, 2002.

67 "On Election Night, Hearne": Interview with Thor Hearne, January 30, 2003.

68 "McCaskill concluded": Audit Report of the Missouri State Auditor, May 26, 2004.

Chapter Five

72 "They discovered men burning ballots": Interview with Kay Daly, November 13, 2000.

73 "There is a lot of abuse": *San Antonio Express-News*, April 4, 2004.

73 "Former representative Debra Danburg": Glenn R. Simpson and Evan Perez, *Wall Street Journal*, December 19, 2000.

75 "Gilberto Quezada": *San Antonio Express-News*, April 9, 2004.

Chapter Six

78 "Michael New, a postdoctoral fellow": *Wall Street Journal*, November 14, 2002.

81 "Maka Duta had bought": Interview with Dewey County auditor Adele Enright, October 12, 2002.

85 "Democratic operatives ran": Byron York, *National Review*, December 23, 2002.

87 "Local Republican leaders": Interview with David Norcross, June 30, 2004.

90   "These practices prompted": *Wall Street Journal*, October 16, 2002.
91   "Senator Daschle made": KELO-TV, October 25, 2002.
92   "Senator Tim Johnson": *Sioux Falls Argus-Leader*, December 23, 2002.
92   " 'Democrats charged Republicans' ": Interview with Ron Williamson, December 3, 2002.
94   "Voters can show": Interview with South Dakota secretary of state Chris Nelson, June 11, 2004.

Chapter Seven

96   "Despite warnings from the states' ": *Honolulu Advertiser*, May 28, 2000.
97   "Cayetano even accused": Interview with Lowell Kalapa, Tax Foundation of Hawaii, February 20, 2000.
98   "At her urging, the state senate": Interview with Senator Colleen Hanabusa, February 18, 2000.
101 "VIP hired two retired FBI agents": Interview with Deborah Phillips of Voting Integrity Project, March 31, 2000.
106 "He subsequently lost his right": Interview with Ed Medeiros, February 20, 2000.
106 "PBN suddenly changed its position": Interview with Malia Zimmerman, May 20, 2000.
107 "They also refused a request": Interview with Governor Linda Lingle, May 3, 2003.

Chapter Eight

111 "Paper ballots were so abused": Paul O'Donnell, *Wired* magazine, January 2004.
112 "She became convinced": Michael Shnayerson, *Vanity Fair*, April 2004.
113 "Andrew divided the people": Speech to Maryland Association of Election Officers, June 9, 2004.
115 "One side sees a security": Interview with Bev Harris, June 24, 2004.
115 "But breakdowns don't equal": Interview with Susan Zevin, July 19, 2004.
116 "who has spent eighteen years": *Chronicle of Higher Education*, April 23, 2004.
117 "Roman Buhler, a former": Interview, July 19, 2004.
119 "Diebold's problems soon": Interview with Bev Harris, June 24, 2004.

119 "Diebold spokesman": Interview with David Bear of ES&S, June 26, 2004.

120 "An internal memo leaked": Michael Shnayerson, *Vanity Fair*, April 2004.

122 "Sequoia is indeed": Interview with Alfie Charles, Sequoia vice president, July 5, 2004.

126 "It began in 1980": Interview with Bob Urosevich, founder of ES&S, March 3, 2000.

128 "A special election to fill": Interview with Florida secretary of state Glenda Hood, February 19, 2004.

129 "Eschberger also admitted": Dan Turner, *Shreveport Times*, November 30, 2003.

129 "In 1998, Sandra Mortham": Associated Press, October 6, 2002.

Conclusion

131 "Early this year, Marsha": Interview with Warren Olney, July 14, 2004.

133 "its lead Democratic sponsor": Interview with Senator Chris Dodd, April 15, 2002.

134 "In 2002, when the outcome": Interview with Colorado secretary of state Donetta Davidson, December 11, 2002.

135 "To cast a normal ballot": Interview with Missouri secretary of state Matt Blunt, December 10, 2003.

137 "Opposition to photo ID laws": *Wall Street Journal*, March 13, 1997.

138 "Eye-popping examples": *Reader's Digest*, August 1997.

139 "State senator David Jordan": *Jackson Clarion-Ledger*, February 20, 2004.

140 "If the initiative had passed": Interview with Jon Caldera, Independent Institute, September 3, 2003.

140 "She compares it to": Interview with Minnesota secretary of state Mary Kiffmeyer, May 4, 2004.

141 "'His view is that voters'": Interview with Garry South, Gray Davis campaign advisor, November 18, 2003.

143 "trial lawyers were extremely active": *Wall Street Journal*, November 6, 2002.

143 "thirteen House Democrats": *San Francisco Chronicle*, July 9, 2004.

145 "Some efforts are under way": Interview with former Virginia Board of Elections chairman Cameron Quinn.

146 "During a bitter recount": *Orange County Register*, April 20, 1997.

149 "The problem is that most states": Interview with Captain Sam Wright, July 19, 2004.

152 " 'The more rules are settled in advance' ": Interview with Indiana Elections Division co-director Brad King, July 19, 2004.

Index

Aberle, Steve, 82
absentee ballots, 4, 5, 8, 41–55;
  California, 41, 42; Colorado, 41;
  costs of, 54–55; Hawaii, 101–2;
  Miami, 5, 47–50; military, 32,
  149–50; neglect of, 12; "no-
  excuse," 42, 45–47; Oregon, 41,
  42–43; permanent, 42, 51; as
  privilege, 49; reforms, 145–45;
  and turnout, 43, 141; Utah, 42;
  vulnerabilities of, 46–47; Wash-
  ington, 42, 55
Academy of Florida Trial
  Lawyers, 143
ACLU, 16, 28
Advanced Voting Solutions, 121
African Americans, 11, 12, 20, 64,
  65; disfranchisement concerns,
  12, 21, 27, 29–33, 142, 148
Aiken, Ann, 43
Albano, Gene, 101
Albowicz, Kay, 144
Aldisert, Ruggero, 43
aliens. *See* noncitizens
Allen, David, 111
Allen, Francis, 22

Alm, Steve, 104
Amador, Miguel, 48
America Coming Together (ACT),
  68–70
American Conservative Union, 19
American Enterprise Institute, 34,
  41
Andrew, Joe, 113–14
Annan, Kofi, 12, 143
Arakaki, Dennis, 104
Arizona, 120, 138
Arkansas, 127–28
Ashcroft, John, 7, 58
Association of Trial Lawyers of
  America, 143

Baker, Evelyn, 58, 59–60, 62, 63
Baker, Miller, 42
Baltimore, 5
Barnes, Gene, 125
Barnett, Mark, 17, 82, 88, 90
Baron, Fred, 142–43
Barondo, Catherine, 67
Barry, Dave, 27
Bartling, Jack, 67–68
Bear, David, 119

163

Maine, 42
Malcolm, Ellen, 69
Mangeri, Gina, 107
Martinez, Guadalupe, 73
Maryland, 120
Mas, Jorge, 48
Massachusetts, 119
Mazo, Earl, 6
McAuliffe, Terry, 13, 79
McCaskill, Claire, 68
McClosky, Frank, 19
McCollum, Bill, 35
McCormack, Connie, 139, 144
McCuen, Bill, 128
McGovern, George, 90
McIntyre, Rick, 19
Medeiros, Ed, 105–6
media, 5, 8–9; bias in reporting,
    32; *Boston Globe*, 28, 44; *Chicago
    Tribune*, 80; *Christian Science
    Monitor*, 80; CNN, 28; *Denver
    Post*, 141; Florida early calls,
    33–34; Florida recounts, 28;
    FOX News, 27, 33, 120; on
    Hawaii scandals, 102, 104,
    105–7; ignoring problems, 97,
    153; *Indianapolis Star*, 24; *Insight*
    magazine, 61; *Las Vegas Review-
    Journal*, 22; *Los Angeles Times*,
    28, 141; *Miami Herald*, 5, 7, 32,
    49, 50, 70; *National Review*, 84,
    86; *Newsweek*, 80; *New York
    Times*, 28, 137; *Pacific Business
    News*, 105–7; *Palm Beach Post*,
    31, 32; pressure on, 84, 99,
    106–7; on same-day registra-
    tion, 141; *San Francisco Chroni-
    cle*, 141; *San Jose Mercury News*,
    123; *Sioux Falls Argus-Leader*, 79,
    80; *60 Minutes*, 4, 46; *St. Louis
    Post-Dispatch*, 58, 65, 66; *USA
    Today*, 28; *U.S. News & World
    Report*, 54; *Vanity Fair*, 118, 126;
    vote suppression by, 33–34;

Wall Street Journal, 28, 78, 97,
    106–7; *Washington Post*, 80;
    Washington Times, 32, 33, 80
Mekler, Margaret, 65
Mexico, 4–5
Meyer, Delvin, 84
Miami: mayoral elections, 32,
    47–50; provisional voting, 134
Miami Herald, 5, 7, 32, 49, 50;
    Pulitzer Prize, 49, 70; racism
    charge against, 50
MicroVote General Corporation,
    124–25
military ballots, 32, 149–50
Milwaukee, 5
Minaii, Brian, 101
Mississippi, 121, 138–39
Missouri: ACT voter registration,
    68–70; military ballots, 149–50;
    polling hours lawsuit, 61; pro-
    visional voting rules, 135–36;
    swing state, 57, 58–59, 69; *see
    also* St. Louis
Moffett, Toby, 47
monitors, 9, 46; electioneering by,
    97; interference by, 86–87; U.N.,
    12, 143
Montegomery, Nona, 66
Moody's, 97
Moore, Michael, 27–28, 33, 153
Mortham, Sandra, 129
"Motor Voter Law," 4, 23–25, 45,
    64, 141
Mrvan, Frank, Jr., 19–20
Murphy, Austin, 8, 44

NAACP, 16, 28, 137
Nance, Earl, Jr., 64
Nassau County (N.Y.), 6, 20
National Association of State
    Election Directors, 145
National Commission on Federal
    Election Reform, 43, 44
National Review, 84, 86

138–39; and *politiqueras*, 73; "racism" charges, 8, 50, 64, 70, 74, 83, 91–92, 93–94; in St. Louis, 64

Rasmussen, Scott, 17

Rasmussen Research, 2, 5, 11, 16–17, 136

rationalization of fraud, 7

Ray, J. K., 72

Ray, John, 74

Raymond, Allen, 21

Reagan, Ronald, 145

Redenbaugh, Russell, 30

Reed, Morris, 137

Reed, Ralph, 28

reforms, 2–3; of absentee voting, 145–46; audits, 129, 147; civics education, 145; counting procedures, 148; death registry, 146; election boards, 147; FEAC, 150–51; Help America Vote Act (HAVA), 2, 46, 66, 118, 133–34, 137; ID requirement, 3, 5, 46, 88, 93–94, 136–39; investigative powers, 146–47; military ballots, 149–50; officials' pay, 152; poll watchers, 147; poll worker training, 2, 144–45; provisional voting, 133–36, 140; as "racist," 8, 13, 25, 70, 74; registration lists, 133; same-day registration, 134, 139–41; vendor investigations, 147–48; voter education, 152; Voting Integrity Initiative, 7; Voting Integrity Project, 42–43, 101–3, 104, 106

Renne, Louise, 15

Reno, Janet, 6, 48, 142

Republican National Committee, 6, 13, 20–21, 113

Republican Party, 6–7, 19–22; fraud concerns, 12–18

Rhode Island, 127

Ridge, Tom, 150

Robio, Mike, 52

Rodriguez, Ciro, 8, 71–72, 74–75

Rodriguez, Geronimo, 71

Romero, Mable, 82

Rose, Melody, 52–53

Rossi, Alberto, 49

Rove, Karl, 53

Russell, Lance, 88

Sabato, Larry, 5, 7, 21, 41

Salas, Luis, 72

Sammon, Bill, 32, 33

Sanchez, Loretta, 24

San Francisco Board of Supervisors, 15, 28

San Francisco Chronicle, 141

San Jose Mercury News, 123

Saranita, Karen, 5

Sazama, Noma, 83, 84

Schreier, Karen, 90

Schumer, Chuck, 66

Schwarzenegger, Arnold, 16

Scott, Clifford, 78

Secure Electronic Registration and Voting Experiment (SERVE), 150

Segawa, Ross, 100, 101

September 11 attack, 1, 14

Sequoia Voting Systems, 121–23; kickbacks, 123; security problems, 123

Shamos, Michael, 115, 116

Shelley, Kevin, 118–19

Shelton, Rodney, 69

Sherbet, Bruce, 73

Shrewsbury, James, 65

Simon, Roger, 54

Simpson, Glenn R., 7, 41

Sioux Falls Argus-Leader, 79, 80

60 Minutes, 4

Slom, Sam, 97

Smith, Linda, 105

Smolka, Richard, 54

Soaries, DeForest B., 150–51